THE STEWARDSHIP OF THE MYSTERY

ALL THINGS IN CHRIST

T. AUSTIN SPARKS

Published by MercyPlace Ministries

MercyPlace is a licensed imprint of Destiny Image®, Inc.

Distributed by

Destiny Image® Publishers, Inc.
P.O. Box 310
Shippensburg, PA 17257-0310

ISBN 0-9707919-6-8

For Worldwide Distribution
Printed in the U.S.A.

This book and all other Destiny Image, Revival Press, MercyPlace, Fresh Bread,
Destiny Image Fiction, and Treasure House books are available at
Christian bookstores and distributors worldwide.

For a U.S. bookstore nearest you, call **1-800-722-6774**.
For more information on foreign distributors, call **717-532-3040**.
Or reach us on the Internet:
www.destinyimage.com

CONTENTS

PREFACE TO SECOND EDITION

This is a volume of messages given in Conference. They are retained in their spoken form. It is important that the reader should remember this, and the attitude should be rather that of one who is listening to, and watching, a speaker, than that of one who is taking account of literary style. The ground covered is comprehensive; no one subject is dealt with very fully....

The messages are in harmony with—if only a poor echo of—the heart-expression of the Apostle who provides the title—"Whom we proclaim, admonishing every man and teaching every man...that we may present every man perfect [complete, entire] in Christ; whereunto I labor..." (Colossians i. 28, 29). May this ministry be prospered unto that end.

T. A. S.
Forest Hill,
London.
1964

ONE

THE PURPOSE OF THE AGES

"...No one knoweth the Son, save the Father..."
(Matthew xi. 27).
"...It was the good pleasure of God...to reveal his Son in
me..." (Galatians i. 15, 16).
"...I count all things to be loss for the excellency of the
knowledge of Christ Jesus my Lord..." (Philippians iii. 8).
"That I may know him..." (Philippians iii. 10).
"Making known unto us the mystery of his will, accord-
ing to his good pleasure which he purposed in him unto
a dispensation of the fulness of the times, to sum up all
things in Christ..." (Ephesians i. 9, 10).

That little clause in verse 10 is the word which will govern our meditation—*all things in Christ.*

These Scriptures speak for themselves. As we listen to the inner voice of the Spirit in these fragments of the Divine Word, surely we shall begin to feel a sense of tremendous meaning, value and content. We should feel like people who have come to the doors of a new realm full of wonders—unknown, unexplored, unexploited.

THE NECESSITY FOR REVELATION

We are met at the very threshold of that realm with a statement which is calculated to check our steps for the moment, and if we approach with a sense of knowing or possessing anything already, with a sense of contentment, of personal satisfaction, or with any sense other than that of needing to know everything, then this word should bring us to a standstill at once: "...no one knoweth the Son, save the Father...." Maybe we thought we knew something about the Lord Jesus, and that we had ability to know; that study, and listening, and various other forms of our own application and activity could bring us to a knowledge, but at the outset we are told that "...no one knoweth the Son, save the Father...." All that the Son is, is locked up with the Father, and He alone knows.

When, therefore, we have faced that fact, and have recognized its implications, we shall see that here is a land which is locked up, into which we cannot enter, and for which we have no equipment. There is nothing in us of faculty to enter into the secrets of that realm of Christ. Then following the discovery of that somewhat startling fact of man's utter incapacity to know by nature, the next fact that confronts us is this: "...it was the good pleasure of God...to reveal his Son in me...." While God has all that locked up in Himself, in His own possession, and He alone has the knowledge of the Son, it is in His heart, nevertheless, to give revelation. And, given the truth that we are so utterly dependent upon revelation from God, and that all human faculty and facility is ruled out in this respect, since such revelation can only be known by a Divine revealing after an inward kind, we are making it to be very evident that everything is of grace when we renounce all trust in works, when we turn away from self-sufficiency, self-reliance, from all confidence in the flesh, and any pride of advance and approach.

Read these two passages in the light of what Paul was when known as Saul of Tarsus, before the Lord met with him, and afterward as Paul the Apostle, and you will gain something more of their force. Saul of Tarsus would have called himself a master in Israel, one well learned in the Scriptures, with a certain strength of self-assurance, self-confidence, and self-sufficiency in his apprehension and knowledge of the oracles of God. Even such a one as he will have to come to the recognition that none of that is of avail in the realm of Christ; where he realises that he is utterly blind, utterly ignorant, utterly helpless, altogether ruled out, and needing the grace of God for the very first glimmer of light; to come down very low, and say: "...it was the good pleasure of God...to reveal his Son in me...." That is grace.

That marked the beginning; and for this present meditation we are considering the unexplored fulness of what God has Himself placed within His Son, the Lord Jesus, actually and in purpose, as being the object of His grace toward us. His grace has led Him to seek to bring us by revelation into all that knowledge which He Himself possesses as His own secret knowledge of His fulness in His Son, the Lord Jesus. *All things in Christ.*

PAUL'S REVELATION OF CHRIST

It is never our desire to make comparisons between Apostles, and God forbid that we should ever set a lesser value upon any Apostle than that which the Lord has set upon him; yet I think that we are quite right in saying that, more than any other, Paul was, and is, the interpreter of Christ; and if we take Paul as our interpreter, as the one who leads us into the secrets of Christ in a fuller way, we mark how he himself embodies and represents that of which he speaks. It is the man himself, after all, and not just what he says which brings us to Christ in fuller and deeper meaning.

The thing that has been very much pressing upon my own heart in this connection is Paul's ever-growing conception of Christ. There is no doubt that Paul's conception of Christ was growing all the time, and by the time Paul reached the end of his earthly life, full, and rich, and deep as it had been, Paul's vision of Christ was such as to lead him to cry even at that point, "That I may know him...." Yes, at the beginning it had pleased God to reveal His Son in him, but at the end it was still as though he had known nothing of Christ. He had come to discover that his Christ was immeasurable beyond his thought and conception, and he was launched into eternity with a cry on his lips: "That I may know him...."

I believe (and not as a matter of sentiment) that will be our eternal bliss, the nature of our eternity; namely, discovering Christ. Paul, as we have said, had a great knowledge of Christ. At best here we find ourselves shriveling into insignificance every time we approach him. How many times have we read the letter to the Ephesians! I am not exaggerating when I say that if we have read it for years, read it scores, hundreds, or even thousands of times, every sentence can hold us afresh each time we come back to it. Paul knew what he was talking about. Paul's conception was a large one, but even so he is still saying at the end, "That I may know him...." I do not think we shall know Christ in fulness immediately we pass into His presence. I believe we are to go on—governed by this word, "the ages to come"—discovering, discovering, exploring Christ. That ever-growing conception of Christ was the thing which maintained Paul in life, and maintained Paul's ministry in life. There was never any stagnation with him. He never came to any point or place where there was the suggestion that now he knew. What he seems to say is this: "I do not know anything yet, but I see dimly, yet truly, with the eye of the spirit, a Christ so great, so vast as to keep me reaching out, moving on. I press on; I leave the things which are behind; I count all things as refuse for the excellency of the knowledge of Christ Jesus, that I may know Him." In this growing conception of Christ, Paul moved a long way from the position of the Jewish teacher, or of the Jew himself at his best.

Paul began with the Jewish conception of the Messiah, whatever that was. It is quite impossible to say what the Jewish conception of Christ was. You have indications of what they expected the Messiah to be and to do, but there is nothing to indicate exactly what their conception of the Messiah was in fulness; it was undoubtedly a limited one. There is a great deal of uncertainty betrayed by the Jewish thought beyond a certain point about their long-looked-for Messiah. Their Messiah represented something earthly and something temporal; an earthly kingdom and a temporal power, with all the earthly and temporal advantages which would accrue to them as people on this earth from His kingdom, from His reign, from His appearing. That is where we begin in our consideration of Paul's conception of Christ. This Jewish conception, it is true, did not confine the thought of blessing to Israel alone, but allowed that Messiah's coming was, through the Jews, to issue in blessing to all nations, yet it was still earthly, temporal, limited to things here. If you read the Gospels, and especially Matthew's Gospel, you will see that the

endeavour of these Gospels, so far as Jewish believers were concerned, was to show that Christ had done three things.

Firstly, how that He had corrected their ideas about the Messiah.

Secondly, how that He had fulfilled the highest hopes that
could have been theirs concerning the Messiah.

Thirdly, how that He had far transcended anything that ever
they had thought.

You must remember that these Gospels were never written
merely to convince unbelievers. They were written also to believers,
to help the faith of believers by interpretation. Matthew's Gospel,
written as it was at a time of transition, was written in order to interpret and confirm faith in Christ by showing what Christ really was,
what He really came for, and in that way to correct and adjust their
conceptions of the Messiah. Their conceptions of Him were inade-
quate, distorted, limited, and sometimes wrong. These records were
intended to put them right, to show that Christ had fulfilled the highest, and best, and truest Messianic hopes and expectations, and had
infinitely transcended them all. You need Paul to interpret Matthew,
and Mark, and Luke, and John; and he does it. He brings Christ into
view as One in whom every hope is realised, every possibility
achieved. Were they expecting an earthly kingdom, and deliverance
and blessing in relation thereto? Christ had done something infinitely better than that. He had wrought for them a cosmic redemption; not a mere deliverance from the power of Rome or any other
temporal power, but deliverance from the whole power of evil in the
universe—"Who delivered us out of the power of darkness, and
translated us into the kingdom of the Son of his love" (Colossians
i. 13). Matthew had particularly stressed the fact of the kingdom, but
the Jewish idea of the kingdom with which he was confronted was so
limited, so earthly, so narrow. With a new emphasis Paul, by the Spirit, brings into view the nature and immensity of the kingdom of the
Son of God's love.

Now we can see something of what deliverance from our enemies means. We shall not follow that through, but pass on with just
that glimpse of it. Such an unveiling as this was a corrective. It
revealed a fulfilment in a deeper sense than they had expected, but it

was a transcendence of their fullest hope and expectation. Paul inter-preted the Christ for them in His fuller meaning and value. He him-self had begun on their level. Their conception of Christ had been his own. But after it pleased God to reveal His Son in him a continuous enlargement in Paul's knowledge of Christ began through an ever-growing unveiling of what He was.

Of course, as Saul of Tarsus, Paul never believed that Jesus of Nazareth was the Messiah. This takes us a step further back in his conception. He believed that Jesus was an impostor, and so he sought to blot out all that was associated with Him in the world.

Paul, then, had to learn at least two things. He had to learn that Jesus of Nazareth was the Messiah, but he also had to learn that Jesus of Nazareth far transcended all Jewish conceptions of the Mes-siah, all his own ideas, all his own expectations as bound up with the Messiah. He not only learned that He was the Messiah, but that as Messiah He was far, far greater and more wonderful than his fullest ideas and conceptions and expectations. Into that revelation he was brought by the grace of God.

THE PROGRESSIVENESS OF REVELATION AS ILLUS-TRATED IN PAUL

I do not think the point needs arguing, for it is hard to dispute that there are evidences of progress in Paul's understanding and knowledge of Christ, and it is clear that progress and expansion and development in his knowledge of Christ led to adjustment. Do not misunderstand. They did not lead to a repudiation of anything that Paul had stated, nor to a contradiction of any truth that had come through him, but they led to adjustment. As his knowledge of Christ grew and expanded Paul saw that he had to adjust himself to it.

This is a point at which many have stumbled, but it is a matter about which we should have no fear. There are so many people who are afraid of the idea that such a man as the Apostle Paul—or any man in the Bible who was Divinely inspired—so utterly under the power of the Holy Spirit should ever adjust himself according to new revelation. They seem to think that this necessarily means that the man changes in such a way as to leave his original position and more or less repudiate it. It does not mean anything of the kind.

Take an illustration. Paul's letters to the Thessalonians were his first letters. In those letters there is no doubt whatever that Paul expected the Lord to return in his lifetime. Mark his words: "...we that are alive, that are left unto the coming of the Lord...." (I Thessalonians iv. 15). In his letter to the Philippians, Paul has moved from that position, while in his letters to Timothy that expectation is no longer with him: "For I am already being offered, and the time of my departure is come. I have fought the good fight, I have finished the course..." (II Timothy iv. 6, 7). He had anticipated Nero's verdict. He knew now that it was not by way of the rapture that he himself was to go to glory. Are we to say that these two things contradict one another? Not at all! In going on with the Lord, Paul came into fuller revelation about the Lord's coming, and of his personal relationship thereto, but this did not set aside or change any fact of doctrine which had been expressed earlier in his letters to the Thessalonians. All that had been set forth there was fully inspired, given by the Holy Spirit, but it was still capable of development in the heart of the Apostle himself, and as he saw the fuller meaning of the things that had come to him earlier in his life, so he found that in practical matters he had to adjust himself. No fresh revelation, nor advance in understanding, ever placed him in the position of having to repudiate anything that had been given him by revelation in earlier days. It is a matter of recognizing that these differences are not contradictions but the result of progressive, supplemental revelation, enlarging apprehension, clearer conception through going on with the Lord. Surely these are evidences that progress in Paul's understanding and knowledge led to adjustments.

THE ETERNAL PURPOSE OF GOD IN HIS SON

Now the great effect of Paul's discovery concerning the Lord Jesus on the Damascus road was not only to reveal to him the fact of His Sonship (he undoubtedly discovered there that Jesus of Nazareth was the Son of God, as his words in Galatians i. 15, 16 show), but to lift Christ right out of time and to place Him with the Father in the "before times eternal." That does not perhaps for the moment appear to be very striking, but it is a very big step toward what the Lord wants to say to us. Christ has been lifted out of time. The "time" Christ, that is, His coming into this world in time, becomes something like a parenthesis; it is not the main thing. It is the main thing if we look at the whole in the light of the fall and need for recovery, but not the main thing from the Divine standpoint originally. I want you to grasp this, because it is at this point that we come into that greatest of all revelations that have been given to us concerning the Lord Jesus. This effect of his experience on the Damascus road, this lifting of Christ right out of time and placing Him in eternity, came in Paul's conception to be related to eternal purpose, and in eternal *purpose* there was no fall and no redemption. That is, so to speak, a bend down in the line of God through the ages. God's line was to have gone straight without a bend, without a break, but when it came to a certain point, because of certain contingencies which were never in the *purpose*, that line had to go down, and then up and on again. The two ends of that line are on the same eternal level. You may, if you like, conceive of a bridge across that bend, and of Christ thus filling the bend, so that what was from eternity is not interrupted at all in Him; it goes on *in Him*. The coming to earth and all the work of the Cross is something other, the result of a necessity by reason of these contingencies; but in Christ from eternity to eternity the purpose is unbroken, uninterrupted, without a bend. There is no hiatus in Christ. This came to be related to purpose. That is a great word of Paul's: "According to the eternal purpose which he purposed in Christ Jesus our Lord" (Ephesians iii. 11); "...called according to his purpose" (Romans viii. 28). These are eternal conceptions of Christ, and this purpose, and these Divine counsels were related to the universe, and to man in particular. Let us get across that bridge for a moment, leaving the other out; for I want you to notice the course that the letter to the Ephesians takes. The letter begins with eternity. It says much of things that were before the world was, and it comes back to that point. Just in between it speaks of redemption, and it never speaks of redemption until it has the past eternity in view.

Redemption comes in to fill up that gap and then we go on to eternity again.

Now just leave the gap for a moment. Of course it concerns us tremendously and we shall have to come back to it, because everything is bound up with redemption so far as we are concerned in the eternal purpose; but leave it for a moment and turn your attention in this other direction. It is stated definitely and clearly that the whole plan of God without redemption was completed in those eternal counsels concerning His Son, Jesus Christ, and in that plan the ages were created: "...the fulness of the times..." is the phrase used here in our translation.

I have heard such phrases in the New Testament as these interpreted as being the dispensations as we now know them in the Bible; the dispensation of Abraham, the dispensation of the Law, the dispensation of Grace. I wonder if that is right? Mark this expression: "...through whom also he made the ages" (Hebrews i. 2 RVM). Let us think again. Are we right in saying that applies to what we call the dispensations as they are shown to us in the Bible? Without being dogmatic about it, I have a question. Are we to say that in those eternal counsels of God, in relation to the eternal purpose of God concerning His Son, a dispensation of Law had a place, an age like the Old Testament age, those periods of time from Adam to Abraham, Abraham to Moses, Moses to David, David to the Messiah? Are those the ages referred to? Did God create those in relation to the eternal purpose? Remember all this creative work was in, and through, and unto His Son, according to *the eternal purpose*.

There are ages upon ages yet to come. There are marks through eternity which are not "time" marks in our sense of the word, but represent points of emergence and development, of progress, increase, enlargement. Had you and I been born on the Day of Pentecost, and were we then to have lived through until the return of the Lord (that is a dispensation according to this world's reckoning and order) we should never have discovered all the meaning of Christ. We should have discovered something and have reached a certain point in the knowledge of Christ, but we should then want another age under different conditions, to discover things which it would never be possible to discover under the conditions of this life; and when we had made good that next possibility, probably beyond that there would be new possibilities. There will be no stagnation in eternity—"of the increase of his government...there shall be no end..." (Isaiah ix. 7).

Now leave the sorry picture of this world's history from the fall to the restitution of all things aside, and you have the launching of ages in which all God's fulness in Christ could be revealed and apprehended progressively, on through successive ages, with changing and enlarging conditions, and facilities, and abilities. That is the meaning of spiritual growth. Our own short Christian life here, if it is a right one, moving under the power of the Holy Spirit, is itself like a series of ages in brief. We start as children, and acquire what we can as children. Then we come to a point where we have increased capacity, where our spiritual senses are exercised. This again issues in a larger apprehension of Christ, and then a little later, as we have gone on, we still find these powers enlarging, under the Holy Spirit, and as the powers enlarge we realise there is more country to be occupied than ever we imagined. As children we thought we had it all! That is, of course, one of the signs of childhood and of youth. The saving thing in our old age is that we recognise there is a vast realm ahead of us to beckon us on and to stop us from settling down. That is eternal youth!

Thus, leaving the whole of this broken-down state in the creation, you can see the creating of ages in Christ, by Christ, through Christ, according to God's eternal purpose that all things should be summed up in Him; not just the "all things" of our little life, of our individual salvation, but the "all things" of a vast universe as a revelation of Christ, all being brought by revelation to the spiritual apprehension of man, and man being brought into it. What a Christ!

That is what Paul saw; and this may well be summed up in his own words: "...the excellency of the knowledge [that knowledge which excels] of Christ Jesus my Lord." It is Paul the aged saying, "that I may know Him." Christ is lifted right out of time, and time, so far as Christ was concerned, was only related to eternity by the necessity of redemption unto the eternal purpose.

We must break off here for the time being, but in so doing let me say this, that with his ever-growing conception of Christ, there was a corresponding enlargement in his conception of believers. Believers came to assume a tremendous significance. The saving of men from sin, death, and hell, and getting them to Heaven, was as nothing compared with what Paul saw as to the significance of a believer now. All that which he has seen concerning Christ in His eternal purpose—eternal, universal, vast, infinite—now relates to believers: "Even as he chose us in him before the foundation of the world, that we should be…unto the praise of his glory…" in the ages to come (Ephesians i. 4, 12). Believers also are lifted out of time, and are given a significance altogether beyond anything here. We shall have to speak further of that.

There was a third thing. He was able rightly to apprise the range and place of redemption. Redemption could be seen in its full compass and as being something more than what is merely of time. It is called "eternal redemption." Redemption is something more than the saving of men and women from sin and their sinful state. It is getting behind everything to the ultimate ranges of this universe, and touching all its powers; linking up with the eternity past and the eternity yet to be, and embracing all the forces of this universe for man's redemption. Paul is able rightly to apprise the meaning, value, and range of redemption, and also to put it in its right place, and that is important.

Now these are big things. They all need to be broken up, and the Lord may enable us to do this, but if you cannot grasp what has been said you will be able to appreciate this, that Christ is infinitely bigger than you or I ever imagined. That is the thing that comes to us so forcibly through Paul. He started with a comparatively small Jewish Messiah; he ended with a Christ so far beyond all that ever he had yet seen or known, that his last cry is, "That I may know him…" and that will take all eternity. What a Christ!

It is Christ who will lift us out, Christ who will set us free; but let me say this, that it will not be by His coming and putting His hands under us and lifting us out, but by being revealed in our hearts. How did Paul come out of his narrow Jewish conceptions about the

Messiah? Simply by the revelation of Christ in him, and as that revelation grew his liberation increased. There were some things which he did not shake off for a long time. He clung to Jerusalem almost to the last. He still had a longing for his brethren after the flesh, and made further attempts for their deliverance on national grounds. But at last he saw the meaning of the heavenly Christ in such a way as to make it possible for him to write the letter to the Ephesians, and the letter to the Colossians, and then Judaism as such, Israel after the flesh, ceased to weigh with him. It was the revelation of Christ which was emancipating him, leading him out, freeing him all the time. In that way Christ is our Deliverer and Emancipator. It is just the Lord Jesus that we need to know. Everything small will go as we see Him. Everything of earth and time will go as we see Him, and in the background of our lives there will be something adequate to keep us through difficult and hard times. We shall see the greatness of Christ and the corresponding greatness of our salvation "according to the eternal purpose...."

Two

The Manifestation
of the Glory of God

Reading: Hebrews i.

As the first thing in this meditation upon Christ, we have been occupied with the ever-growing conception of Him that marked the life of the Apostle Paul. We saw first how that Paul as a Jew had himself shared the very earthly and narrow conception of Messiah so common to his race, with all its thought of a temporal kingdom, privilege, and position, and how for him this conception came to be shattered by the revelation which he had of the Lord Jesus while journeying on the road to Damascus.

This crisis marked the beginning of an ever-growing knowledge of Christ. There Paul had learnt, not only that Jesus of Nazareth was Himself the long-expected Messiah, but that He was also the Son of God, who from before times eternal had been in the bosom of the Father. Christ was thenceforth to him no longer just a figure of time; and we marked how that by further revelation this fact came to be related to what Paul frequently calls purpose; the purpose of God, the Divine counsels—"…who worketh all things after the counsel of his will…" (Ephesians i. 11). That is related to the "before times eternal," and in that purpose, in those Divine counsels from eternity, very many things are found to which Paul refers. We saw that these Divine counsels (this eternal purpose) concern the universe, and man in particular, and that both the universe and man are gathered up into His Son: "…according to his good pleasure which he purposed in him unto a dispensation of the fulness of the times, to sum up all things in Christ, the things in the heavens, and the things upon the earth" (Ephesians i. 9, 10). That led us to consider a point which requires perhaps stating afresh, or at least a reiteration, to which therefore we now proceed.

THE PURPOSE OF THE AGES

These eternal counsels (this eternal purpose of God) represent the straight line of God through the ages, and as we are considering them have nothing to do with redemption. That is another line, an emergency line. We were saying that this fulness of the times, of the ages or seasons, represents God's eternal method of unfolding His fulness, and of bringing men into that fulness. They are stages of growth, of progress, of development concerning His Son, and, as we have said, all this was intended to be a straight line through the ages. These other ages of which we read, the ages of this world according to present conditions, are quite another line and introduce another expression of purpose. They were brought in, if we may put it figuratively or imaginatively, in this way: The Godhead in counsel laid the plan for all the future ages of the ages from eternity to eternity, and in that plan everything was clear and straightforward. There would be a progressive unveiling of God in the Son, and a progressive bringing of the universe into that fulness. But then God reached a point where He had to say, because of His foreknowledge (we speak imaginatively): "But We know what will happen. We know that at a certain point the man whom We create will fail, will break down. That will mean a long period of disorder, disruption, chaos, and We must provide for that." There the whole plan of redemption was introduced, and the Lamb was slain from before the foundation of the world. That is another line of purpose. Thus the ages of this present world had to be introduced; the age before Law, from Adam after the fall to Moses, an age governed by certain things; then the age of Law up to Christ; then the age or the dispensation of the Church. These were not in the original plan. It is necessary to say that, because, were it otherwise, it would make God responsible for sin, and you might say: Well, if God had planned all that, the fall was bound to be; God had to bring about the fall! But that is not true. None of us would lay it to God's charge that He had planned the fall in order to make redemption necessary. That is another line of purpose, of planning according to the foreknowledge of God. The first line of purpose was not that, and, as we said, you start on a level and then reach a point where, because of failure and sin, there is a dip in the line, and in that dip, in that gap the whole story of redemption is seen. Christ bridges it and links up the first purpose, and its realisation, from eternity past to eternity to be. Coming in the likeness of sinful flesh, but without sin, the Redeemer stands in the gap and carries the purpose of the ages straight on in Himself. The present dispensations are, shall we say, subsidiary in their nature, and were brought in because of an emergency. God never intended it to be like that. Let us be quite clear on that point.

The fact which stands out clearly for us, and which is one of tremendous value, is that God intended that there should be ages, times, periods in which there should be increasing revelation, manifestation, and apprehension of Himself. Perhaps it sounds speculative, but let us ask: Now what would have happened if the fall had never taken place? If man had survived his testing in the garden and had not broken down, what would have happened? I believe man would have grown, grown, grown in his apprehension and knowledge of God, grown in his personal expression of God. God would have thus secured a progressive, ever-developing expression of Himself and, seeing that God is what He is, there would have been no limit to this; it could have gone on through successive ages, with movements in this universe into ever greater fulnesses of God.

We are not speaking of individual man but of collective man. That is what God intends, and that is what will be. Bridge the gap. Get right across the whole gap that has been filled by the redemptive program, and take the matter up at the point where redemption is complete. Get back on to God's first level, triumphant over the enemy, and take things up there. What are you going to have? You are going to have a progressive, ever-growing expression of the fulness of God displayed in ages, in ever-widening circles of the revelation of God. It is not possible to comprehend the fulness of God. It will take eternity to express that.

All that fulness is in Christ; and our point at the moment is, how great is that fulness! What a Christ we have! It will take eternity to discover Christ. There is no small meaning about that statement. We recall the words of the Lord Jesus Himself: "...no one knoweth the Son, save the Father...." That, of course, does not merely imply a question of identification, that no one knows who Christ is except the Father. It signifies what Christ stands for in the history of this universe, all that He is in His position in it. I believe it is unto an understanding of that that the Lord is calling us. The Lord wants us to come to a new understanding and apprehension of His Son, Jesus Christ, and that apprehension is our way out, our way up, our way to fulness. This, as we have said, came to be related to purpose, to Divine counsels concerning the universe, and man in particular.

THE PERSONIFICATION OF THE DIVINE THOUGHT IN A BEING

Its central meaning was in relation to a type of created being called man, and man is an expression of Divine thought, an image and likeness of something conceived in the mind of God. These are the eternal counsels issuing in eternal purpose, the counsel of His will. Now let us break that up.

God thought thoughts. You and I think thoughts, thoughts that correspond to our mental constitution, our nature, our make-up. One thinks after one manner because he is made that way, another after another manner because he is made that way. Our thoughts are the expression of our nature, our constitution, our disposition; in a word, our make-up. "For as he thinketh in his heart, so is he..." (Proverbs xxiii. 7 KJV). The thought is the man in essence. God thought thoughts. Those thoughts were God in essence. They were the projected mind of what God is like, what God thinks, what God is. Those thoughts were projected toward an object called man; that man should be an expression, a living personification of God's thoughts.

God desired desires. Now of man it is equally true that as a man desires in his heart so is he. We desire according to our inclinations, according to our preferences, according to what we feel to be best. Our desires express ourselves. God's desires are an expression of His own nature, His own being, His likeness. Those desires were created in man, that man should be a living embodiment of God's heart, God's desire; desiring one desire with God, thinking one thought with God; one in mind, one in heart with God.

God willed a will. Our wills always betray us. What we will is the unveiling, the disclosing of what we are after, what we mean, what we intend. That is true of God. God willed a will, and that will was God, after the nature of God, the essence of God's nature, disposition, intention. That will of God was focused upon man, that man should embody the will of God and express it in personal living expression; living in the will of God, living by the will of God, his whole being gathered up in one inclusive and positive expression: Thy will, O God! There was to be a created being called "man" after that order, to be in that moral-spiritual sense the image of God, the likeness of God. This was not to share Deity, but to have the moral nature of God; the spiritual nature of God in mind, and heart, and will reproduced in man, expressed in a creation. That is where God's thought rested, and that is God's purpose. He would have it to be fruitful and multiply and replenish the earth; to grow and expand; morally and spiritually to reach out into all spiritual realms and fill the universe. Moral forces are forces which go far beyond the individual in which they rest or are centered.

THE LIE AND ITS OUTWORKING

Now you can see why Satan sought to capture man, and why he went about it in the manner that he did. It is as though he said: "Set aside God's mind, God's will, God's desire!" In other words, "Accept mine instead!" Now what have you? The expansion of that thing from a man to a universe! Those moral forces which are other than God intended are cosmic forces now. They have gone far beyond the individual, far beyond the family to a race, and out beyond a race to all the encircling realms of the cosmos. There is a will other than God's impregnating the very atmosphere. There are other desires, other feelings, other thoughts, all against God.

See, then, the awful alternative. See how far-reaching this matter is. Had man been true to God's expressed thoughts, His expressed desires, His expressed will; had man, in other words, been true to himself as out from the hand of God, which was to be true to God, this whole world, this whole cosmos to-day would be an expression of God's thought, desire, and will. What a world! What a universe! But what is it now? Such a thing as a thousand leagues of nations will never set it right. Man has let loose something in this universe by his treachery, his complicity with God's enemy, which must work itself out until this creation is an expression through and through of that which has revolted against God: and it will compass its own doom. What a difference! It is working out in that way. Try to arrest war. How futile! It is the working out of that thing: "...only there is one that restraineth now, until he be taken out of the way" (II Thessalonians ii. 7). When that restraint is fully removed, you will see this whole creation as one leavened lump, seething with anarchy and self-destruction. God never intended that.

Do you see God's thought for man, God's intention, God's purpose? It was to express Himself through the universe. With this dispensation and creation just the opposite is expressing itself, and will do so until the end. This is not God's thought, God's desire, God's will; this is anarchy. It is against God, against His purpose, against His creation. Blessed be God, we are out of that creation, because we are in Christ, and Christ bridges the gap. He takes up the original intention. In Him you have God's thoughts, God's desires, God's will perfectly expressed, and we are in Him, a new creation in Christ Jesus. Now what is our business? To learn by the Holy Spirit to live after God's thoughts, according to God's desires, and in God's way. That lies ahead of us for our further consideration. It is only hinted at for the moment.

CONFORMITY TO CHRIST ESSENTIALLY MORAL AND SPIRITUAL

You see the result was intended to be a created corporate race as an expression of that which was, in essence, God. I do not mean Deity, I mean that which was intended in moral essence; the kind of thoughts God thinks, the kind of desires God desires, the kind of will God wills. God intended a created corporate race as an expression of Himself in that sense. You see it in Christ. You have the meaning of Christ when you see all that. This is what Christ means. This is the interpretation of Christ. How great a Christ!

Paul sees Him lifted altogether out of time, sees Him related to God's purpose; His express image, the effulgence, the very essence of God. Yes, His Deity included the moral essence of God. The expression of God in an Image morally constituted after God, that is Christ.

It is a great thing to see Christ, and then to see that we were chosen in Him to be like that, "...conformed to the image of his Son" (Romans viii. 29). The first representation of that thought, that mind, that heart, that will of God, was the Son; and the Son was *not created but begotten*. Man was created to be conformed to the image of the Son, but the Son was not created. He was the only begotten of the Father; unique, standing alone, inclusive, conclusive.

Those are not mere words. In the creation according to God there will be nothing but what is of Christ. It is important to realise that. That will govern a good deal that we may have yet to say. Thank God, you and I will not be as we are. It is not to be Christ *and* us; all is to be Christ. That is to say, Christ will be so corporately expressed that, the question of Deity apart, the moral and spiritual essence of Christ will utterly govern every other unit in the universe. It will be Christ in that sense; one great universal, collective, corporate Christ! Yes, there will be multitudes which no man can number, yet so conformed to the image of Christ that, looking at any one or all of these, spiritual conformity to Christ will be seen. We are not saying that Christ is to lose His individuality, to be absorbed in some inclusiveness where all His own personal distinctiveness ceases; we are saying that, when conformed to His image, we are to be as one great person, the Body of Christ perfected, a corporate and collective expression of what Christ is.

Paul refers to that when, with tremendous faith representing a tremendous victory and ascendancy, he said: "...we henceforth know no man after the flesh..." (II Corinthians v. 16). It represents a victory of no mean order. In our dealings with the Lord's children, for instance, Paul means that, notwithstanding all that we may find of inconsistency and failure, because of what they are by nature, we are to focus all our attention upon Christ in them, and because they are Christ's, and He is in them, make His indwelling the ground of all our relations with them, keeping our eyes off the other altogether; we are to know them after Christ and not after the flesh. It will not be difficult in the ages to come, for then there will be nothing but what is of Christ in us. We shall see Christ in one another, we shall be fully conformed to His image. The Lord hasten that day!

What a Christ! See His position in God's purpose. See the universal, eternal Christ, embracing all, excluding all; excluding all that in character is unsuitable to God, and not out from Him, and including in Himself as the Son all that has become conformed to His image. Christ inclusive of creation, for all things were created for Him. They will be His, but as morally purged and made suitable to Him. That is why He refused them at the hands of the Devil. "...All these things will I give thee, if thou wilt fall down and worship me" (Matthew iv. 9). He disdains the offer. Costly as the path would be— and He knew it—He would not be caught by that proposal. In effect He says: "I will have them, but I will have them when all the trouble and the heartbreak have gone." That is the effect of it; the whole creation included in Christ: but what a Christ!

One of the great governing factors and features of the new creation in Christ is deathless life. In the present creation at its best death reigns, decay reigns. Deathless life! There is no death at all in that new creation.

All the ages are included in Christ. Yes, there are ages yet to be—"That in the ages to come..." (Ephesians ii. 7). Those ages are being included in Christ. That means that Christ will give them their character. They are to take their nature, their character from Christ, and inasmuch as they are ages, it means that progress, development, increase, expansiveness, extensiveness is all a matter of going on and enlarging unto Christ. The ages are made for Him, and the ages to come are for the showing forth in us of God in Christ. All the Divine fulness is in Christ. These are statements in the Word.

The Gift of Eternal Life

In the creation of man at the first one great factor was suspended. Perhaps it was the most important factor, and it was suspended pending man's probation and testing. What was it that so entirely depended upon how man issued from the probation and testing? It was eternity of life; life from the Divine standpoint; what God means by life. This was suspended pending the trial of man, and it introduces a further great factor of the Word of God—namely, the revelation of God. This represents the great governing question in history from Adam onward. The great governing question is this: In whom can that which is called eternal life dwell? We know that eternal life is not mere duration of being. It is a kind of life; it is God's life, Divine life, the life of the ages. In whom can that life dwell? That is the great governing question of history. The answer to the question is Christ: "In *him* was life..." (John i. 4). He is the life. But then, we behold Him not only as personal, individual, separate, but corporate; the creation in Christ.

That concludes the first stage and begins the next. Up to that point everything, so far as this present time is concerned, is one great question. In this redemption period, brought in as a second line of Divine arrangement, the whole matter of our response to God's call, of our acceptance of Christ, and of union with Him is in the balance. One big question hangs over this dispensation: Who will respond? To many He has had to say, "...ye will not come to me..." (John v. 40). The question is settled once the life is within; you have started at that point where Adam broke down, and have immediately been lifted out of the gap, out of the bend; you have been brought up there in Christ and have come right into the straight line of the eternal purpose which, in its realisation, will be a universe full of Christ: "Unto a dispensation of the fulness of the times, to sum up all things in Christ...."

Are you asking what this is all about? If you are not yet clear it can be put into very few words. It is to bring the greatness of Christ into view, that is all. Now we need that there should happen to us, in the grace of God, what happened to this man who came into this ever-growing, inexhaustible conception of Christ. We recall his own words: "...it was the good pleasure of God...to reveal his Son in me...." You may have heard all this: it may have sounded more or less wonderful; you may know the truth, in an intellectual way; but there is all the difference between that and the way in which Paul knew it. Paul's way of knowing brings emancipation.

Have you ever seen a fly in a bottle? Round and round it goes, beating itself from side to side, rising, falling, until you really ache as you watch that fly. You saw it rise a little and your hopes rose with it, and then you saw it go down, trying to find a way out, beating itself to death. Then up, climbing and reaching the top, out and away! That is the difference.

You and I with all our head knowledge, our mental knowledge of a great spiritual realm, find it a hopeless thing if in reality we are living down in this creation. To-day it would be easy to despair, to drop down into things as they are. Look out into the world for prospects for the Church, prospects for the Gospel, prospects for the Lord. Look at the state of the Church itself. Bring the letter to the Ephesians down into this world! You will give it up and say: "It is a wonderful conception, but impossible." Try to realise it down on this level and you beat yourself to despair. Note Paul as he looks out over the churches which he had seen brought into being and sees them breaking up, and the men for whom he had suffered turning against him. Paul would have despaired in his heart, had he been living down here. What were the prospects in such conditions? But he got up into the heavenlies in Christ Jesus and saw that this was a heavenly thing, an eternal thing. Read the Ephesian letter again and mark how it starts: "Blessed be the God and Father of our Lord Jesus Christ, who hath blessed us with every spiritual blessing in the heavenly places in Christ: even as he chose us in him before the foundation of the world, that we should be holy and without blemish before him in love: having foreordained us unto adoption as sons through Jesus Christ unto himself, according to the good pleasure of his will, to the praise of the glory of his grace, which he freely bestowed on us in the Beloved: in whom we have our redemption through his blood, the forgiveness of our trespasses, according to the riches of his grace" (Ephesians i. 3-7).

These are the words of a man with his life-work tumbling to pieces and all his old friends for whom he had sacrificed himself turning against him. What has he seen? The eternity, the universality of Christ, *all things in Christ*. Paul is not living in this world now, but living in Christ. It is the only way out. It is the way of life, the way of hope, the way of assurance in a day like this when things close down. Christ is the way out: "...in the heavenly places *in Christ*..."; "...chose us *in him* before the foundation of the world...." Again we say: What a Christ!

Let us dwell much upon the Lord Jesus, for everything for us is in Him.

THREE

A MAN AFTER GOD'S HEART

Reading: Psalm lxxxix. 19, 20; Acts xiii. 22; Hebrews i. 9; I Samuel xiii. 14.

The Bible abounds with men. It abounds with many other things, with doctrine, with principles; but more than anything else it abounds with men. That is God's method, His chosen method, His primary method of making Himself known. These men who were in relationship with God, with whom God was associated, bring distinctive features into view. Not in any one man is the whole man acceptable, every feature to be praised, but in every man there are one or more features that stand out and distinguish him from all others, and abide as the conspicuous features of that man's life. Those outstanding distinctive features represent God's thought, the features which God Himself has taken pains to develop, for which God laid His hand upon such men, that throughout history they should be the expression of certain particular traits.

Thus we speak of Abraham's faith, of Moses' meekness. Every man is representative of some feature wrought into him, developed in him, and when you think of the man the feature is always uppermost in your mind. Our attention is drawn, not to the man as a whole, but to that which marks him in particular. So by one apostle we are called to recollect the faith of Abraham, while another will bid us remember the patience of Job. These features are God's thoughts, and when all the features of all the men are gathered up and combined, they represent Christ. It is as though God had scattered one Man over the generations, and in a multitude of men under His hand had shown some aspect, some feature, some facet of that one Man, and that one Man is able to say, "Ye search the scriptures, because ye think that in them ye have eternal life; and these are they which bear witness of me" (John v. 39). There is a Man spread over the Bible, and all who have come under God's hand, have been apprehended for the purpose of showing something of His thought, which in its fulness is expressed in His Son, the Lord Jesus. Recognising that, we are better able to appreciate the words we have just read, which in the first instance related to David, but are clearly seen to reach beyond to a greater than David. Read again Psalm lxxxix and you cannot fail to see that two things merge into one another: "...I have laid help upon one that is mighty; I have exalted one chosen out of the people." You have to look for a greater than David for the complete expression of that. In the words "I have laid help upon one that is mighty" we have one of the great foundations of our redemption. A greater than David is here. David in those principal features of his life under God's hand was an expression of God's thought concerning Christ. You cannot say that of David's life as a whole. You cannot carry the statement, "I have found...a man after My heart..." through the whole of David's life, and say that when David was guilty of this and that particular thing which marred his life this was after God's heart. We have to see exactly what it was, in and about David, which made it possible for God to say that he was a man after His own heart. It was just that which indicated Christ, pointed to Christ. It is only that which is Christ which is after God's heart.

THE DIVINE PURPOSE FROM ETERNITY

"...Jehovah hath sought him a man after his own heart..." (I Samuel xiii. 14). Remembering our previous meditations, we shall find a large setting for a statement like that. It speaks of the creation of man, of the Lord seeking to have a man-race, a corporate man in whom His own thoughts and features are reproduced in a moral way. The Lord has ever sought Him that man. It was the seeking of such a man that led to the creation. It was the seeking of such a man that led to the Incarnation. It is that seeking of a man which has led to the Church, the "one new man." God is all the time in quest of a man to fill His universe; not one man as a unity, but a collective man gathered up into His Son. Paul speaks of this man as "...the church, which is his body, the fulness of him..." (Ephesians i. 22, 23). That is the fulness, the measure of the stature of a man in Christ. It is the Church which is there spoken of, not any one individual. God has ever been in quest of a man to fill His universe.

THE LIKENESS IS MORAL AND SPIRITUAL

God thinks thoughts, desires desires, and wills wills, and those thoughts, and desires, and wills are the very essence of His moral being, and when He has thus reproduced Himself in this sense, He has a being constituted according to His own moral nature; the man becomes an embodiment and personification of the very moral nature of God; not of the Deity of God, but the moral nature. You know what it is in life to say that anything or anyone is after your own heart. You mean they are just exactly what you think they are and what you want them to be for your own complete satisfaction. The man after God's heart is like that to Him.

DEVOTED TO THE WILL OF GOD

There is a third thing which defines that to some degree, which puts its finger upon the root of the matter. What is the man after God's heart? What is it that God has sought in man? The verse in Acts tells us: "...who shall do all My will" (Acts xiii. 22). If you look at the margin you will see that "will" is plural: "...all My wills"—everything that God desires, everything that God wills, the will of God in all its forms, in all its ways, in all its quests and objectives. The man who will do all His wills is the man after God's heart, whom God has sought. The words are spoken, in the first place, of David. There are several ways in which David as a man after God's heart is brought out into clear relief.

Firstly, David is set in striking contrast with Saul. When God had deposed and set aside Saul, He raised up David. Those two stand opposite to one another and can never occupy the throne together. If David is to come, then Saul must go. If Saul is there, David cannot come. That is seen very clearly in the history, but let us note that in this we are confronted with basic principles, not merely with what is historic and to do with persons of bygone days. Before God there are two moral states, two spiritual conditions, two hearts, and those two hearts can never be in the throne together, can never occupy the princely position at the same time. If one is to be prince, or in the place of ascendancy, of honour, of God's appointment, the other heart has to be completely put away. It is remarkable that even after David was anointed king there was a considerable lapse of time before he came to the throne, during which Saul continued to occupy that position. David had to keep back until that regime had run its course, until it was completely exhausted, finished, and then put aside.

It would be a long, though profitable study, to go over Saul's inner life as shown by his outward behaviour. Saul was governed by his own judgments in the things of God. That is one thing. When God commanded Saul to slay Amalek—man, woman, beast, and child; to destroy Amalek root and branch, it was a big test of Saul's faith in God's judgment, God's wisdom, God's knowing of what He was doing, God's honour. If God commands us to do something which on the face of it would seem to deny something in God's own nature of kindness, and goodness, and mercy, and we begin to allow our own judgment to take hold upon God's command and to give another complexion to the matter, to take obedience out of our hearts, we have set our judgment against God's command. In effect we have said: "The Lord surely does not know what He is doing! Surely the Lord is not alive to the way His reputation will suffer if this is done, the way people will speak of His very morality!" It is a dangerous thing to bring our own moral judgment to bear upon an implicit command of the Lord. Saul's responsibility was not to question why, but to obey. We recall Samuel's word to Saul: "...Behold, to obey is better than sacrifice, and to hearken than the fat of rams" (I Samuel xv. 22). The man after God's heart does all His wills, and does not say: "Lord, this will bring You into reproach! This will bring You into dishonor! This will raise serious difficulties for You!" On the contrary, he replies at once: "Lord, You have said this; I leave the responsibility for the consequences with You, and obey." The Lord Jesus always acted so. He was misunderstood for it, but He did it.

Saul was influenced in his conduct by his own feelings, his own likes and dislikes, and preferences. He blamed the people, it is true, but it was he himself who was at fault after all. It was his judgment working through his sentiments. In effect he said: "It is a great pity to destroy that! Here is something that looks so good, that according to all standards of sound judgment is good, and the Lord says destroy! What a pity! Why not give it to God in sacrifice?" Now we know that it is true of the natural man that there are these two aspects, a good side and a bad. Are we not, on our part, often found saying, in effect, "Let us hand the good to God! We are quite prepared for the very sinful side to go, but let us give the good that is in us to the Lord." All our righteousnesses are in His sight as filthy rags. God's new creation is not a patchwork of the old; it is an entirely new thing, and the old has to go. Saul defaulted upon that very thing. He reasoned that the best should be given to God, when God had said, "Utterly destroy."

The man after God's own heart does not make blunders like that. His interrogation of himself is: "What has the Lord said?" No place is given to any other inquiry: "What do I feel about it? How does it seem to me?" He does not say: "It is a great pity from my standpoint." No! The Lord has said it, and that is enough. God has sought Him a man who will do all His wills.

So we could pursue the contrast between Saul and David along many lines. We are led to one issue every time. It all points in one direction. Will this man surrender his own judgments, his own feelings, his own standards, his entire being to the will of God, or will he have reservations because of the way in which *he* views things and questions God?

AN UTTER REJECTION OF THE FLESH

There is another way in which David stands out as the man after God's own heart, and it is this with which we are especially concerned, and with which we will conclude this meditation. It is that which is to be noted in the first public action of David in the valley of Elah. We refer, of course, to his contest with Goliath. This first public action of David was a representative and inclusive one, just as the conquest of Jericho was with Israel. Jericho, as we know, was representative and inclusive of the conquest of the whole land. There were seven nations to be deposed. They marched round Jericho seven times. Jericho, in spiritual and moral principle, was the embodiment of the whole land. God intended that what was true of Jericho should be true of every other conquest, that the basis should be one of sheer faith; victory through faith, possession through faith.

David's contest with Goliath was like that. It gathered up in a full way everything that David's life was to express. It was the comprehensive disclosure or unveiling of the heart of David. He was a man after God's own heart. God's ground of approval in His choice of men is shown to us in His words to Samuel with reference to another of Jesse's sons: "...Look not on his countenance, or on the height of his stature...Jehovah looketh on the heart" (I Samuel xvi. 7). In the case of David, the heart that God had seen is disclosed in the contest with Goliath, and it was that heart which made David the man after God's own heart all the rest of his life. What is Goliath? Who is he? He is a gigantic figure behind whom all the Philistines hide. He is a comprehensive one, an inclusive one; in effect, the whole Philistine force; for when they saw that their champion was dead they fled. The nation is bound up with, and represented by, the man. Typically what are the Philistines? They represent that which is very near to what is of God, always in close proximity, always seeking to impinge upon the things of God; to get a grip, to look into, to pry, to discover the secret things of God. You will recall their attitude toward the Ark when it came into their hands. They were ever seeking to pry into the secrets of God, but always in a natural way. They are called "uncircumcised." That is what David said about Goliath: "this uncircumcised Philistine." We know from Paul's interpretation that typically that means this uncrucified natural life, this natural life which is always seeking to get a grip on the things of God apart from the work of the Cross; which does not recognise the Cross; which sets the Cross aside, and thinks that it can proceed without the Cross into the things of God; which ignores the fact that there is no way into the things of the Spirit of God except through the Cross as an experienced thing, as a power breaking down the natural life and opening a way for the Spirit. There is no possibility whatever of our knowing the secrets of God except by the Holy Spirit, and the Holy Spirit "was not" (we use the word in the particular meaning of John vii. 39) until Calvary was accomplished. That must be personal in application, not merely historic. The uncircumcised Philistines simply speak of a natural life which comes alongside the things of God, and is always interfering with them, touching them, looking into them, wanting to get hold of them; a menace to that which is spiritual. Goliath embodies all that. All the Philistines are gathered up into him. David meets him, and the issue, in spiritual interpretation, is this, that David's heart is going to have nothing of that. He sets himself that all things shall be of God, and nothing of man. There shall be no place for nature here in the things of God, but this natural strength must be destroyed. The Philistines become David's lifelong enemies, and he theirs.

Do you see the man after God's heart? Who is he? What is he? He is a man who, though the odds against him be tremendous, sets himself with all his being against that which interferes with the things of God in an "uncircumcised" way. That which contradicts the Cross of the Lord Jesus, that which seeks to force its way into the realm of God other than by the gate-way of the Cross is represented by the Philistine. Who is this uncircumcised Philistine? David's heart was roused with a mighty indignation against all that was represented by this man.

That constitutes a very big issue indeed. It has not merely to do with a sinful world. There is that in the world which is opposed to God, positively set against God, a sinful state that is recognised and acknowledged by most people. That is all against God, but that is not what we have here. This is something else that is to be found even amongst the Lord's people, and which regards nothing as too sacred to be exploited. It will get into an assembly of saints in Corinth and call for a tremendous letter of the Apostle about natural wisdom, the wisdom of this world expressing itself as the mentality even of believers, and thus making the Gospel of none effect. This spirit that is not subject to the Cross creeps in and associates itself with the things of God, and takes a purchase upon them. It is not so much that which is blatantly, obviously, and conspicuously sinful, as the natural life which is accounted so fine according to human standards. The Lord's people have always had to meet that in one form or another. Ezra had to meet it. Men came and proffered their help to build the House of God: and how the Church has succumbed to that sort of thing! If anybody offers their help for the work of the Lord, the attitude at once taken is: "Oh, well, it is help, which is what we want; let us have all the help we can get!" There is no discrimination. Nehemiah had to meet it. There is some help that we are better without. The Church is far better without Philistine association. That is the sort of thing that has assailed the Church all the way through. John, the last surviving Apostle, in his old age writes: "...but Diotrephes, who loveth to have the preeminence...receiveth us not" (III John 9). You see the significance of that. John was the man of the testimony of Jesus: "I John...was in the isle that is called Patmos, for the word of God and the testimony of Jesus" (Revelation i. 9). The great word of John's writings is "life": "In him was life..." (John i. 4); "...this life is in his Son" (I John v. 11). Diotrephes could not bear with that. If Christ is coming in, Diotrephes, who loveth to have the pre-eminence, must go out; if he that loveth to the pre-eminence is coming in, then Christ is kept out.

The man after God's own heart is the man who will have no compromise with the natural mind; not only with what is called sin in its more positive forms, but all that natural life which tries to get hold of the work of God and the interests of God, to handle and to govern them. This has been the thing that has crippled and paralysed the Church through the centuries; men insinuating themselves into the place of God in His Church.

You see what David stands for. He will take the head off that giant. There has to be no compromise with this thing; it must go down in the name of the Lord.

THE PRICE OF LOYALTY

Now notice this, that for his devotion David had to suffer. This man, who alone saw the significance of that with which he had to do, this man who alone had the thoughts of God in his heart, the conceptions of God, the feelings of God, the insight of God; this man who alone amongst all the people of Israel in that dark day of spiritual weakness and declension was on the side of God, seeing things in a true way, has to suffer for it. As he came upon the scene, and, with his perception and insight into what was at stake betraying itself in his indignation, his wrath, his zeal for the Lord, began to challenge this thing, his own brethren turned upon him. How? In the cruelest way for any such man, the way most calculated to take the heart out of any true servant of God. They imputed wrong motives. They said in effect: "You are trying to make a way for yourself; trying to get recognition for yourself; trying to be conspicuous! You are prompted only by personal interests, personal ambitions!" That is a cruel blow. Every man who has come out against that which has usurped God's place in any way, and stood alone for God against the forces that prevail, has come under that lash. To Nehemiah it was said: "You are trying to make a name for yourself, to get prophets to set you on high and proclaim through the country that there is a great man called Nehemiah in Jerusalem!" Similar things were said to Paul. Misrepresentation is a part of the price. David's heart was as free from any such thing as any heart could be. He was set upon the Lord, the Lord's glory, the Lord's satisfaction, but even so, men will say: It is all for himself, his own name, his own reputation, his own position. That is more calculated to take the heart out of man than a good deal of open opposition. If only they would come out and fight fairly and squarely in the open! But David did not succumb; the giant did! May the Lord give us a heart like David's, for that is a heart like His own.

We see in David a reflection of the Lord Jesus, who was eaten up by zeal for the Lord's House, who paid the price for His zeal, and who was, in a sense above all others, the Man after God's own heart.

Four

PUTTING ON THE NEW MAN

Reading: Romans v. 12, 15-19; Ephesians iv. 13, 20-24; Colossians iii. 9-11.

Here the Word says we have put off the old man, or more literally, that we have laid down or laid aside the old man. The same word is found in Hebrews xii. 1—"Therefore…lay aside every weight, and the sin which doth so easily beset us…." We have laid down, or put off, the old man. So often those words are used by us in a merely personal connection. We speak of "our old man"; by which we mean this sinful nature of ours which rises up under provocation. That aspect, of course, is included in the initial act of faith's repudiation, but that is not all that is meant by the statements before us. It is included; but what we have here is something very much more.

THE SIGNIFICANCE OF THE TERM "OLD MAN"

Romans v. explains what is meant. The old man is a racial order, represented by its racial head, Adam. It is an order. That corporate, collective Adam, as apart from God, having departed from God, is a kind of order which can no longer be accepted by God, which has passed out of God's thought and God's acceptance, and stands contrary to His mind. That is the order into which we are born, and to which all that we are by nature belongs, and it is spoken of as a corporate, collective entity. It is important to remember that, not only is the Body of Christ one, but the Body of Adam is one; that is, that all in Adam are also a corporate being. It is a man, a kind of man, a type of man expressed world-wide; and we are said to have put off that man, the old man; we have laid him aside, laid him down.

We have laid him in the grave in the same way that we lay a corpse there. The body of one who has departed this life is laid aside. It is no longer the place in which he dwells. He has laid aside that body, and we follow up and likewise lay it aside. Now as believers we have put off, have laid aside the Adam type, the Adam order, the Adam system, this one great collective man of a certain kind, of a certain order.

The New Man

Then it is further said that in Christ we have put on the new man. That also is often thought to be a merely personal affair, an individual matter. That is to say, the new man in our conception is a kind of new personal life and nature. That is true, but it is far more than that. In the letter to the Ephesians, the Apostle is speaking of the new man which is the Church, "the Christ" as it is literally expressed in First Corinthians xii. 12. Christ is one with all His members, as the Head joined to the body, all the members making one body, one new man. It is a collective, corporate man, a man of a new order which is not Adam, but Christ: "where...Christ is all, and in all" (Colossians iii. 11). Before it was Adam who was all, and in all, but now in this new creation it is Christ who is seen to be all, and in all. The Apostle well expresses what is meant when he writes: "But ye did not so learn Christ; if so be that ye heard him, and were taught in him, *even as truth is in Jesus*" (Ephesians iv. 20, 21). It is a great embodiment of Divine truth in a Person, and we are represented as having divested ourselves of the one body, of old Adam, and as having invested ourselves with this body of Christ, with the new man.

(A) The Primary Feature

That includes a good many things. If you look at the context of this passage you will observe some of them. It includes the nature of Christ. That is why, after mention has been made of putting on the new man, the Apostle proceeds almost immediately with words like these, "Be ye therefore imitators of God, as beloved children; and walk in love, even as Christ..." (Ephesians v. 1, 2). The new corporate man is the embodiment of the love of Christ. That is the first thing. This love must have an individual expression, for what is said to be true of the whole body is only so in the degree in which it is found to be true of the individual member. Let us recognise that, when we speak of the Church, or the Body of Christ, or make use of this alternative title, the "new man," we are speaking of that which is the embodiment of Christ's love; and when we say we are putting on, or have put on, the new man, we mean that we have put on the love of Christ.

To walk in love, then, is one thing that is involved. The Body is built up in love; the Body is constituted by love; the Body is the means of expression of Christ's love. If you take the figure and follow it, you will see how impossible it is to escape the fact. Were you to find a body without a head, it might be said that you had found a body; but it would be a very mutilated body! It really could not in the full sense be called a body. The Lord Jesus has not such a Body. For a full expression of the meaning of "body" must have head and members all together, properly adjusted and related. Now Christ cannot be said to be love as the Head, and His members be viewed apart from Him. The Body is one; Christ in expression is inclusive of His members, and that involves a nature. That nature is love: therefore "...as beloved children...walk in love, even as Christ also loved you...."

Love is not the only feature in this new nature. We use it simply by way of indicating that this nature does imply a new Body-disposition. You and I need to be more before the Lord for a Body-disposition. The disposition of this new man is the disposition of love. Let us ask the Lord for the increase of this disposition in the Body of Christ. All that is other than that is still the old man, and he has to be put off. When anything that is not of the love of Christ springs up amongst us as the Lord's people, in any form whatever—and there are many forms of thoughts, and feelings, and words; words of criticism, words of judgment—love has to put it off. If you and I are found with such a thing as a spirit of criticism one toward another, that is of the old man, the old Adam, and he has to be put away. We have to recognise that the Lord has put old Adam in the grave. Then we have to follow up and say: "To the grave you go; you belong there!" The new man, then, speaks of a new nature, and of a new disposition. We all need more of this "new man" disposition, that we may walk in love.

(B) A CORPORATE CONSCIOUSNESS

Then this new man, being corporate and collective, being related and inter-related in this way, represents a life of fellowship. It demands a corporate consciousness which is one of the most important things. In the Lord's purpose everything depends upon this corporate life. The Lord Himself can never reach His end by individuals, and you and I can never reach that ultimate end as individuals. Although it is true that Adam, the old man, is a corporate unity, the consciousness of the old man is not a corporate consciousness; it is an independent consciousness, a divisive consciousness. We must have a corporate consciousness in order to reach God's end. There are quite a number of the Lord's own dear children who remain far too long in a state of spiritual immaturity. They never grow much beyond childhood spiritually. You may know such for years, and find them to be just the same simple children to-day as when you first knew them. Now, it will be said: "It is very right and proper to be a simple child of the Lord!" Well, let us always have a childlike spirit, let us always seek to be of a pure, simple spirit before the Lord, but let us remember that there is a difference between childlikeness and childhood. There is all the difference between keeping that simplicity, purity, openness, teachableness of the child, and a delayed understanding, an overdue ability to grasp spiritual things and to assimilate food for those more advanced in years. The trouble with so many people, or the cause of their own delayed maturity, is that they are merely going their own sweet way; that is, they are butterflies, simply flitting from one thing to another with no corporate life, no related life. A butterfly is quite a pretty thing as it flits about, but there is all the difference between a butterfly and a bee. A bee too may go from one thing to another, but it does so to very good purpose. The bee's life is a corporate life, the butterfly's is not a corporate life; it is an individual life.

Delayed maturity, stunted spiritual growth, is very often due to this lack of a corporate sense of life which is bound up with the life of the Lord's people in a definite and positive way. That is the way of enlargement. That is the law of the new man. We arrest our spiritual growth when we set aside the necessity for a life that is linked with the people of God in quite a definite way. That is a background in Ephesians. The whole of the fourth chapter is devoted to this vital matter. The new man is there set forth as the church, the Body of Christ, and this new man is to grow unto the measure of the stature of the fulness of Christ. It is the corporate man that grows to that stature; individuals cannot do so. Only in relatedness do we move into the fulnesses of Christ.

Beware, then, of missing that very important law of spiritual enlargement. This is what is meant by putting on the new man. We are right, then, in asking the question, "Have we really put on the new man?" Have we really put on a Body-consciousness, a related-consciousness, a fellowship-consciousness that belongs to the new man? It may not always be possible for us to enjoy the immediate, local, geographical fellowship of a large company of the Lord's people, but that is not the point; we are talking about a consciousness.

(c) A Disposition

Again, it is a disposition. It is the setting aside of everything individual, personal, separate, as such, and putting on that consciousness of relationship in which everything is for the Body, and in the Body, and by the Body. It is by this fellowship of spirit that the Lord gains His end and we come to the Lord's end.

It is very sad to see the results of failure to recognise that. There are some, of whose devotion to the Lord we have no question, but the thing that pains us is that they have not grown one fraction of an inch since we first knew them years ago. At least, there is no sign of larger capacity. They are just exactly the same as they were. Such as these are never to be found making a supreme effort for a relatedness of a definite kind with the Lord's people. They flit about from one thing to another, and they say: "I am not going to settle down in any one particular fellowship of the Lord's people! I am going to keep free! I am going to move about and keep in touch with every-thing that there is!" That may be very good from one point of view; and you must not misunderstand and suppose it to be said that we are not to be in sympathetic touch with all that is of the Lord. But there is something else which is necessary to building up, and that is a concrete relationship with the people of God. It is necessary to the Lord for fuller revelation. What do we not owe in the matter of rev-elation to this very thing! For revelation the Lord must have the Body spiritually expressed. It is tremendously important to know that. It is there that the Lord's ministry functions. Ephesians iv is a great ministry chapter. You lose all isolation and departmentalism in ministry when you have the Body in realised expression, when everyone is found occupying some place of spiritual value in the work of the Lord; not according to the technical terms that man is wont to use with reference to such work, but where everyone repre-sents something of spiritual value, where everyone is a minister before the Lord in some way. Whether you recognise it or not, it is a fact, and unfortunately a great deal of loss is suffered because it is not realised how greatly obedience on the part of every one of us affects the issue.

I will tell you how to test it. Is there going to be something per-sonal for the Lord by a corporate means, say a conference? I venture to say that there are not many people who are spiritually associated with that who do not know some aspect of the Devil's rage and pres-sure in connection with it. You do not have to provoke the Devil in any way. It is one conflict and not only are the more evidently responsible individuals in ministry affected, but the conflict reaches to those whom we do not connect with ministry in that specific sense. In our thought we so often limit the ministry to this one expression of it. Those who have ordinary home and domestic duties may haply think of them as something quite other, and not as part of the ministry, but the conflict finds its way in there. It gets into you personal consciousness, into your business, apart from your being in any more immediate way involved in what is going on. It is because you are spiritually related to a testimony, because you have come in a spiritual way into the Body of Christ, recognising what the Body of Christ is. Whether you have understood the truth or not in any large measure, you have put on the new man and you are suffering as a part of one man.

Now that is not only a fact which perhaps we recognise in a painful way, but it is a privilege. Paul said, "Now I...fill up on my part that which is lacking of the afflictions of Christ in my flesh for his body's sake, which is the church" (Colossians i. 24). There in your homes, in your business, in what you would call the back places, you meet with the conflict. It is for the Body's sake. Out there, far away from others, you are meeting the impact. That is the proof that every part of this Body is a partaker in this ministry. The whole is being served by every part in a spiritual way putting on the new man.

Although it involves us in the cost, in the suffering, it equally means that we come into the good and the value; for no few members can come into blessing without all who are in spiritual relationship receiving benefit. If one member suffers, all the members suffer; if one member rejoices, all the members in some way rejoice, in some way come into the good of it.

GOD'S QUEST IS A MAN

You will see that this is very closely related to what the Lord is seeking to bring to us in these days. We are still speaking of it in very general terms, but the presentation of the Lord's mind ought to be very clear to us. It is a man that God is after. That man is represented by His Son, and the Church is His expression as His Body. This new man is the universal manifestation of what Christ is—one Lord, one Life, one Love. It is important, lest you should make a mistake in interpretation, to recognise that there is a difference between the word used in Ephesians and that in Colossians. In Ephesians we read of putting on the new man, in Colossians we read of having put on the new man. In Ephesians the word *kainos* means something that never was before, something altogether new. This Church never was before; this corporate man according to Christ never existed before, it is something new. In Colossians another word is used which simply means "fresh," not necessarily altogether new. You will see the significance of the different word if you look at the context. There is a freshness of mind, a freshness of spirit that is to be a mark of those who are in Christ. But our word at this time has to do with the former word, which is *kainos*, the new man, the man that never was before. There is an old man who was before, and he has to go. Here is another man that never was before, and he has to be put on.

This new man is after God. That takes us back to our previous meditation, God thinking His thoughts, desiring His desires, and willing His wills, all of which express His own nature, and all of which are focused upon a created being called "man": "...that after God hath been created..." (Ephesians iv. 24). That is a marvelous expression. You know how we speak of certain works of men, and use that word. We say, "After Landseer!" We mean that it is a reproduction of Landseer. Now here is a new man which after God is created in righteousness. The Lord teach us the meaning more clearly of so learning Christ.

FIVE

HIS EXCELLENT GREATNESS

Reading: I Kings iv. 1, 7, 20-34; x. 1-9; Matthew xii. 42.

Some of the passages which have provided the background for our meditations have referred very definitely and precisely to the excellence and exceeding greatness of the Lord Jesus. One basic passage of tremendous implication is that which came from His own lips: "...no one knoweth the Son, save the Father...." That is a declaration, in other words, that only the Father knows the Son, knows who the Son is and what the Son is; only the Father knows all that the Son means. Along with that we have the profound statement of the Apostle Paul: "...it was the good pleasure of God...to reveal his Son in me...." That relates to the beginning of his life in Christ Jesus, and it was a revelation which was destined to become so full that after all his years of learning, after all his discovery of Christ, at the end he is still to be found crying from his heart, "...I count all things to be loss for the excellency of the knowledge of Christ Jesus my Lord: for whom I suffered the loss of all things, and do count them but refuse, that I may gain Christ" (Philippians iii. 8). It indicates clearly that even at the end the Apostle recognised that there was a knowledge of Christ still available to him which was beyond anything that had yet come to him, and such knowledge was more precious and more important than all other things. We often sing in one of our hymns, "Tell of His excellent greatness"—"Behold, a greater than Solomon is here."

Our difficulty always will be to comprehend, to grasp, to bring that excellent greatness, that transcendent fulness within the compass of practical everyday life and experience. Yet it is necessary that this should be, and our approach to that fulness must be of such a kind as to render it of immediate value to us; for all that vast range of power and fulness, although so far beyond our comprehension, is yet for our present good and advantage. There are some features in this account of Solomon's greatness which foreshadow this greatness of the Lord Jesus, a greatness which, as we have said, is for our present benefit.

(A) SUPREME DOMINION

We mark that it is said of Solomon that he was king over all Israel and that he had dominion over all the region beyond the river; and a greater than Solomon is here. The first feature, then, is this of his supreme dominion, his excelling lordship, kingship, sovereignty. That is of tremendous practical value. It operated, as we see, in two realms; he was king over all Israel, and he had dominion over all the region *beyond* the river.

Those statements suggest that the Lord Jesus is not only King within the compass of those who acknowledge Him as Lord, His own saved ones, but that, in spite of what may seem, He is King in a far wider sense. We are moving much in the realm of Ephesians in our consideration, and in Ephesians it is the universal sovereignty of the Lord Jesus that is brought before us, not only His relation to the Church. He is Head over the Church which is His Body, He is Lord there, but He is, in addition, far above all rule and authority, principality and power. He is *now* universal Lord. It does not appear like it; everything would seem to contradict the fact; but we need to be given sight to see that the kingship, the lordship, the universal dominion of the Lord Jesus at this present time does not necessarily mean that all are enjoying that lordship, nor that for all within the universe is it a beneficent reign. But even if that be the case, it does not alter the fact. There are other things which also point to the fact in a very positive way.

Of course, our trouble is that we take such short views. We are children of a span of time, and that span of time is of such great importance with us that our view of things is so narrow. If we could but take the long view, and see things from God's standpoint, how different would be the result in our own hearts. In saying that, we have in mind the widespread denial of the kingship, the lordship, the sovereignty of the Lord Jesus Christ. This period of the world's history is called the day of His rejection and there is a verse of a hymn that commences thus:

> *Our Lord is now rejected,*
> *And by the world disowned.*

But it is not so easy a matter to put the Lord Jesus aside. Men may reject, nations may reject, may seek to put Him out, deny Him a place, repudiate His rights, refuse to acknowledge His claims and His lordship, but that does not get rid of Him. God has set His king upon His throne. Of the Son He has said, "Thy throne, O God, is for ever and ever..." (Hebrews i. 8). Nothing can upset that. The attitude of men, the attitude of the world, cannot interfere with that, cannot depose the Lord Jesus. It may be said: "That is a statement, but how will you prove it?" Well, there are evidences. We have evidence that He is Lord, that He is holding things in His own sovereign hand, that *nothing can take His place.*

THE WITNESS OF HISTORY

Look at history and see what has tried to take the place of the Lord Jesus in sovereignty; tried to do what only the Lord Jesus could do; tried to bring about a state of things, to accomplish which is put into the power of the Son alone, and see how far those efforts have succeeded. Anything which seeks to bring about a state of things which the Lord Jesus alone can establish is doomed. You can see it repeated through history again and again. World dominion has been sought by one and another. Things which were ideals, magnificent conceptions for the world, have been attempted, and they have all failed, all broken down. Kingdoms and empires, despots, dictators, monarchs, have risen to a tremendous height, some of them having great sway, but the empire has broken and passed, the reign has broken down. So you have these things coming and going all the way through history; and, mark you, the whole matter is related to the Lord Jesus.

Read the Book of Daniel again, and you will perceive the realm in which we are moving. There you have the prophetic unveiling of world empires; Babylonia, the empire of the Medes and Persians, then that of the Greeks, and on to the great Roman Empire; they all pass in review, and pass away. The lesson of the Book of Daniel is this, that there is but *One* whom God has appointed to be universal Lord, and that no one else can hold that place. Others may go a long way, but they can never gain that place, and so they must pass. We may yet see great powers coming into being, vast ranges of territory under one sway, but all this will pass. The matter is held in the hands of the Lord Jesus. All this endeavour is doomed from its birth to go so far, and then pass out. The Lord Jesus alone can have world dominion. He alone can bring universal peace. He alone can bring prosperity to all nations. That is held in reserve for Him and His reign. Till then there will be fluctuations and variations in world fortunes, but it will all pass.

This passing, this breakdown, this confusion, this deadlock is all because the course of things is in His hands, and He is holding it all unto Himself. He is King! He is Lord! It is a tremendous thing to recognise that the very course of the nations, the very history of this world, is held in the hands of the Lord Jesus unto His own destined end. God has for ever set His Son as the only one to be full, complete, and final Lord of His universe, King of kings and Lord of lords, with a beneficent sway and reign over all the earth. Peace and prosperity is locked up with the Lord Jesus, and He holds the destiny of nations unto that. Men may attempt it of themselves, and they may go a long way to usurp His place, but the end is foreseen, foreshown. He must come whose right it is, and *of His kingdom there shall be no end*. It has commenced in Heaven; it is already vested in Him and held in His hands. That is how we must read history. That is how we must read our daily papers. That is how we shall be saved from the evil depression and despair that would creep into our hearts as we mark the state of things in this world. All is being held by Him to a certain end. The meaning is that *nothing* can take the place of the Lord Jesus.

You can apply that in various ways, and in different directions. It explains the history of the so-called church, the history of Christendom. Why is it that what professes to be of Christ, but in reality is not, breaks down, continually breaks down all the way through history? Simply because it is something assuming the place of Christ, which is not of Christ. Failure is written upon it from the beginning. Everything that is not of Christ is going to break down; and it does break down. Though a thing may begin with Christ and evidence a measure of Christ, immediately it moves beyond the range of Christ and becomes of man, its end is in view.

That is the explanation of things which God has raised up in relation to His Son, things which were pure and true, but of which, because of the blessing resting upon them, men have taken hold. Whenever this has been done the end of these things has come into view, that is, as a spiritual force. Why is this? It has gone beyond Christ, it has gone outside of Christ, and nothing can take the place of Christ. Oh, how necessary it is to abide wholly in Christ, to be wholly of Christ, according to Christ, governed by the Holy Spirit. He operates His sovereignty against the success, the prosperity, the final triumph of anything and everything that is not of Himself, and if we want the sovereignty of the Lord Jesus on our side, then we have to be utterly on the side of the Lord Jesus; otherwise that sovereignty works against us. The world confusion, and the world trouble, and the world despair, is all a mighty evidence that Jesus is Lord, because it is a world that is trying to get on without Him, but cannot do so. No! He says it cannot be done. He says: "I am essential! I am indispensable! If you would have it otherwise, then you must learn that without Me it cannot be done."

We could spend all our time considering Solomon's dominion and kingship. He was king over Israel, and had dominion over all the land beyond the river. But we must pass on to consider another feature in which Solomon foreshadows the excellency of the Lord Jesus.

(B) The Bounty of Solomon's Table

"And Solomon's provision for one day was thirty measures of fine flour, and threescore measures of meal, ten fat oxen, and twenty oxen out of the pastures, and an hundred sheep, besides harts, and gazelles, and roebucks, and fatted fowl" (I Kings iv. 22, 23). That is a great day's feast for Solomon! What does this speak of, if not of the bountifulness of Solomon. This is no mean fare, no starvation diet! "A greater than Solomon is here."

When by the Holy Spirit we really come into the knowledge of the Lord Jesus, there is no need to starve spiritually. Oh, the tragedy of starving believers, with such a King! The tragedy, the unspeakable grief of children of the Lord spiritually starving! The fact is there is a fulness for His people which far excels that of Solomon.

Read the Gospel of John again with this one thought in mind, and you will see how the truth receives confirmation from the earthly life of the Lord Jesus. Take chapter vi, with its great incident of the feeding of the multitude, all leading up to the spiritual interpretation: "I am the bread...." His disciples broke down in faith at one point, and He was amazed: "Do ye not yet perceive, neither remember the five loaves of the five thousand, and how many baskets ye took up? Neither the seven loaves of the four thousand, and how many baskets ye took up?" (Matthew xvi. 9, 10). He was amazed at their failure to understand that in Him was not only enough, but abundance. There is something wrong with us if we have not discovered it to be so. The fulness of Christ is for our spiritual satisfaction. There is abundance of food.

Again, consider not only the pathetic tragedy, but the wicked tragedy of starvation. What is it that is keeping the Lord's people out of fulness? Very largely it is prejudice, the Devil's trick of putting up the barrier of prejudice between the need and the supply. Oh, the wickedness of the Devil in coming in by these works of blinding to starve the Lord's people. There is bread in Christ. He is an inexhaustible fulness for the spiritual life. We know that we shall come to the same position as Paul, when he cried, "That I may know him..."—that is, to a consciousness of there being a knowledge beyond anything that we have yet attained unto, and where everything is counted as nothing compared with that. This is not mere words, it is true. There is bread in the Lord Jesus; there is bread in His house. This is where He is superior to Solomon. There is bread for a mighty host, a company capable of doing greater justice to His fare than ever Solomon's household could do. If they had sat down to his bounty, they could have gone so far and no farther, but our appetite will go on. We have a spiritual capacity which is growing, and growing all the time, unto the fulness of Christ. Solomon's bounty, then, is another feature by which he foreshadows the excellent greatness of the Lord Jesus. We touch but briefly on a third.

(C) THE GLORY OF SOLOMON

The glory of Solomon is proverbial. Even the Lord Jesus spoke of it as being so: "...Consider the lilies of the field, how they grow; they toil not, neither do they spin: yet I say unto you, that even Solomon in all his glory [and they knew what his glory was] was not arrayed like one of these" (Matthew vi. 28, 29). But what was Solomon in his glory compared with the Lord Jesus? What is the glory of the Lord Jesus? Inclusively it is the revelation of the fulness of God, the glory of God in the face of Jesus Christ.

That may not sound very practical, but let us mark that this glory of Solomon was closely associated with his wisdom; his wisdom indicated the nature of his glory. There was something beyond the glory. This glory was not mere tinsel, or mere show, but was the fruit of a great wisdom that God had given him. It was the wisdom of Solomon that issued in his glory and his fame. What may be said of his wisdom? He spoke three thousand proverbs, he wrote many songs; he spoke of trees, and of beasts, and of birds, of creeping things, and of fishes. They are all very practical things. How did he speak of them? He invested everything in the creation with a meaning. If he speaks of trees, he will give you a secret, give a meaning to the trees, from the cedar in Lebanon (trees in the Word of God all have a significance) to the hyssop that springeth out of the wall. We know of what hyssop speaks as we first meet with it away back in Exodus and Leviticus. We know what the cedars of Lebanon stand for, and all the trees in between the two equally bear a meaning. Solomon gave the secret significance, the Divine meaning. Then he spoke of beasts, and we know that the Bible speaks of many beasts, and they all have a significance. He spoke of fowls also, and of creeping things, and of fishes. He unfolded the secrets of the creation, and invested everything in the creation with a deeper meaning. To be able to do that is proof of no mean wisdom.

Wherein is the Lord Jesus superior? Well, after all, Solomon's was only poetic wisdom in those realms. The Lord Jesus has practical wisdom; in this sense, that everything is laid hold of by Him in relation to His purpose, and made to serve that purpose. Oh that we could see and believe that at all times in our experience! So many things come into our lives. What a diversity! What a range! How mysterious some things seem to be! How strange it is that the Lord's own people have so many more experiences, both in number and variety, than anyone else. It seems that almost anything that can happen to a person, happens to a believer. You wonder sometimes, if anything else is possible. Have we not exhausted the whole store of possible experiences? That is how we question. There is not one thing in the life of a child of God but what is controlled and governed by a deeper meaning in relation to His purpose. We recall Paul's statement: "And we know that to them that love God all things work together for good, even to them that are called according to his purpose" (Romans viii. 28). The more accurate translation is, God worketh in all things good. God invests everything with a meaning, for those who love Him, and are the called according to His purpose. The wisdom of God lays hold of everything and gives to it a value. It may be that only eternity will reveal to us the value of some things, but we must believe that, inasmuch as our lives are wholly under His government, there is nothing without a meaning, nothing without a value. His wisdom is governing everything.

It is when we come to realise that, to accept and believe it, that we find rest in our hearts, and find ourselves on the way to gain rather than loss. When we revolt against these things, then we are in the way to rob ourselves of something. But when we come into line with the Lord in these things we find, firstly, rest in our hearts, and then the discipline produces something of value. It is gain, not loss; it is good, not evil. This is wisdom. That is better than having so many poems; it is practical. A greater than Solomon is here! That is the glory of the Lord Jesus. How does His wisdom work out to His glory? You and I go through a painful experience, a mysterious experience; we can see no good in it; we can only see harm in it. We are led to look to the Lord, to believe that although we cannot see, cannot understand, He knows; and we trust Him. We come through the trial, and our eyes are enlightened about the purpose of it, and we worship. Oh, we never saw that such a thing as that could produce this! We never, never imagined that this value could result from it. The thing which seemed to be for our undoing is the thing that has brought us into a greater fulness of the Lord. That is His glory.

Remember that His wisdom is governed by His love. That is a great point with Solomon. It was the heart of Solomon which was behind his wisdom. It was a wise and understanding heart (not brain). Now look at Solomon. Two women bring a babe to him. Solomon is watching. For what is he watching? For something that he knows out of his own experience. Read the story of Solomon's birth. Read that little clause about his mother's special love for him. Solomon was the darling of his mother's heart, and Solomon knew what mother love was. He knew what the love of a mother for her babe was, and he watches those two women. He has the keen eye of a mother or her child upon those two women, and he says to one at his side: "Take this sword and divide the child in two." That does not sound very much like a mother heart; but he is watching. Then he sees the mother heart leap, and hears her cry: "No! I had rather that the other woman had the child than that you should hurt it!" And Solomon knew who was the mother of that child. That is the wisdom of Solomon which is actuated by his love.

Supremely does this characterise the Lord Jesus. Oh, it seems at times that the way He goes to work is hard, but it is actuated by His love. It may be strange and mysterious, but love is in it; there is a great heart behind it all.

When at the direction of Solomon the Ark was brought into the sanctuary, and set there in its appointed place, speaking of the Lord coming into His rest and satisfaction, we are told that this symbolic realisation of the Lord's end in rest was attested from Heaven, and that Solomon turned his face to the people and blessed them. God has come into His rest in His Son, into full satisfaction, and then the Son, in whose face is the glory of God, turns to us in blessing: "…the glory of God in the face of Jesus Christ" (II Corinthians iv. 6). A greater than Solomon is here.

The Lord give us a new apprehension of His Son.

Six

The Heavenly Man—The Inclusiveness and Exclusiveness of Jesus Christ

We have under consideration a phrase from the letter to the Ephesians, "*All things in Christ*": "unto a dispensation of the fulness of the times, to sum up all things in Christ..." (Ephesians i. 10). That is the great general vision that is occupying us, and we will now begin to break it up into its parts.

To begin with, it is supremely important that we should recognise that there is one basic and all-governing factor with God, which is a supreme matter for our knowledge, and that is the inclusiveness and exclusiveness of His Son, Jesus Christ.

Everything intended and required for the realisation of Divine purpose and intention is in, and with, Christ, not only as a deposit, but all *is* Christ. That is the inclusiveness of Christ.

Then, on the other hand, nothing but what is of Christ is accepted or permitted by God in the final issue. That is the exclusiveness of Christ. However God may seem in His patience and long-suffering, in His grace and mercy, to be bearing with much, even in us His people, which is not of Christ; however much He seems for the time being to allow, it is of supreme importance that we settle it once for all that God is not really allowing it. He may extend to us His forbearance, His long-suffering, but He is not in any way accepting what is not of Christ. He has initially said that it is dead to Him, and He is progressively working death in that realm. So that in the final issue, not one fragment anywhere that is not of Christ will be allowed. Christ excludes everything that is not of Himself. That is God's ruling of the matter.

THE CHURCH TO BE WHAT CHRIST WAS AND IS AS THE HEAVENLY MAN

In view of what we have just said, it is of the utmost importance for real effectiveness that we should realise that the Church is intended to be what Christ was, and is, as the Heavenly Man. Only that which is of Christ, the Heavenly Man, is eternally effective. Therefore, the more there is of Christ, the more effectiveness there is from God's standpoint. That means that what was, and what is, true of Him as the Heavenly Man, as to His being, as to the laws of His life, as to His ministry and His mission, is to be true of the Church. (When we speak of the Church, of course, we speak of all the members as forming the Church.)

Do you notice that we are speaking of Christ as the Heavenly Man, and not of His co-equality with the Father in Deity? We are not saying that the Church is to be, in the same sense as Christ, God incarnate, occupying the place of Deity; we are speaking of the Heavenly Man. Christ was, and is, a *Heavenly* Man. The Church in Him is also a Heavenly Man, one "new man." It is not to be thought of as Jew and Greek, circumcision and uncircumcision, bond and free, a combination of earthly elements, of various aspects of human life as here on this earth. These and all other earthly distinctions are lost sight of and set aside, and one "new man" is brought in, where "Christ is all, and in all" (Colossians iii. 11).

Christ has never been, in His essential nature, of the earth. He had a relationship to Israel, a relationship to man here; He has a judicial relationship to this earth, but in His essential nature He never has been earthly. He is the Lord from Heaven. He takes pains to stress the fact, and to keep it clearly in view: "...I am from above..." (John viii. 23).

Now as Christ in His essential nature never was of the earth, neither is the Church. The Church has never been an earthly thing in God's thought. That is where the gap is bridged. Paul takes you right back, and shows you that the Church is in the heavenlies before ever the fall took place. In Christ we are made to bridge the gap created by the fallen ages. Before the world was, Christ existed with the Father, literally and personally. The Church existed in the fore-knowledge of God before the world was, though not literally in the same way that Christ did; that is, this is not a reincarnation, but, in the foreknowledge of God, the Church was as actual before time as it is now, or ever will be. Whenever Paul speaks of the Church, he always speaks of it as though it were complete. He never speaks of a completing of it. Much has to be done to add the members, to bring it to its numerical completeness, and its spiritual and moral com-pleteness and perfection, but while Paul has much to say about spir-itual growth and increase, he yet speaks of the Church as though it were already completed. He is viewing it from the heavenly, eternal, Divine standpoint, from the standpoint of the foreknowledge of God. There in that foreknowledge of God, and that foreordaining accord-ing to foreknowledge, the Church existed as a complete whole with the Father and the Son before times eternal. Then came the break, the gap, the dip down; but in Christ it is bridged, and the Church is seen as a continuous thing in the heavenlies, above it all.

The Church is seen as being literally formed in this dispensa-tion, but it is as immediately translated to Heaven. Immediately we come into Christ, we are seated in the heavenlies in Christ: "But God...when we were dead through our trespasses, made us alive together with Christ...and raised us up with him, and made us to sit with him in the heavenly places..." (Ephesians ii. 4, 6). It does not say that we are to be placed there at some future date. Before ever we believed, we became a heavenly people from God's standpoint. We were cut clear of this world, translated out of this kingdom of dark-ness into the kingdom of the Son of His love, and ceased to be earth-ly, immediately we came into Christ. We are lifted right back on to the level of the original purpose, and linked up with the first thought of God in Christ. We become the corporate Heavenly Man, even as He is the Heavenly Man in person.

We are called upon to recognise our link with the eternal and the heavenly, and to take things up from there. There would not be that terribly anomaly of "worldly Christians," if only this were apprehended. Look at all that has to be dealt with because of failure to keep the testimony pure for the Lord's people. Worldly Christians! What a contradiction to the Divine thought! How impossible it is to accept anything like that! Let us repeat, we are called upon to recognise our link with the eternal and heavenly, and to take things up from there. It is not the case that we are struggling, working, striving to be a heavenly people; now aiming at such a state, and hoping that at some time it will be realised, but we are a heavenly people, and we must take things up from that standpoint.

The convert, the young child of God, must remember that by his union with Christ he becomes entirely a heavenly part of Christ from the first, linked with everything heavenly and eternal. Everything here is to be as out from another realm. That should be kept in view. We should have a very different kind of believer if that were always kept to the fore. That is God's standpoint, God's mind.

This, then, brings us to the point at which that eternal and heavenly relationship is resumed. It is not the commencement but the resumption of Christ of something that was broken off, interrupted, and which ought never to have suffered such an interruption.

NOTHING BUT WHAT IS OF CHRIST ALLOWED BY GOD IN THE ULTIMATE ISSUE

Before we deal with the point of resumption, we will spend a few moments in looking yet further at the implication of what has been emphasised already. Nothing but what is of Christ is allowed by God in the ultimate issue. Now, because that is true, all the activities of God in discipline are introduced and pursued. All the discipline which comes by failure, for example, is followed out. Failure is in the way of God's thought now, a necessity as it were. Lives reach a point, and then are unable to get beyond that point; there is a going on so far in a measure of blessing, and then the state of things changes, the kind of blessing that has been is withheld, and a state of things ensues which has but one issue, that of an absolute necessity for a new position in the Lord. It is not that the Lord blesses what is not of Christ in such a period, but in His grace and mercy He blesses us, in order to lead us on in Christ: then, when we have come to a place where we have a certain knowledge of the Lord, the Lord suspends that outward blessing, and we pass into a time of trial, of conscious failure, defeat, arrest, helplessness, and we are found before long in that realm saying: "My need is of a new place with the Lord, a new experience of the Lord, a new knowledge of the Lord. All that has been, has been very wonderful, but it is as nothing now, and the need now is a new place with the Lord."

That will go on to the end. The experience is not relative to the early stages alone, but continues throughout the course. How many of us have cried, "Lord, we need a new position!" What is this? It is the outworking of this law, that with God nothing but what is of Christ is allowed. Only that which is of Christ can be effective, and our experience means that more of the mixture has to go, and Christ has to take its place. Failure leads to that.

The same thing applies with regard to work, to great movements. The history of a movement is like that of the individual. Even that which has been blessed of God comes to the place where, as a movement, as a collective instrumentality, it knows that the old days have passed, and for that which now obtains, and that which is before, a new position is necessary. Unfortunately so many try to live upon the past, try to go on upon a reputation, a history, and will not confess to the fact that things have changed and that God requires something more. If only they would face up to that, how much more glorious in its effectiveness would be the future, than ever the past has been. But there you have the interpretation of the experience. However, it is apprehended by those concerned, the fact remains that God applies this law, that in the end, when everything has been said and done, and when all these present ages have run their course, in God's ages of the ages there will be nothing but what is of Christ. He is seeking to bring the Church to that goal, to be the fulness of Him that filleth all in all. It cannot be the fulness of Christ while anything else is there.

How manifold is the application of this truth! How many a detail it touches, and how ashamed it should make us! If we really do see it, if it really strikes our hearts, we shall be greatly humbled.

Inwardly we shall feel thoroughly disgusted with ourselves as in the light of this we think of *our* assertiveness, of *our* strength, of *our* activity in the things of God, of all that has been of ourselves in this realm. The putting forth of strength is only effective in the proportion in which it represents a measure of Christ. We puny folk on this earth stand up and think we are of some account! What insignificant people we are if viewed from the heavenlies! The Lord looks down upon us and sees us trying to make names for ourselves in His things; dominating other lives; manipulating, putting our hands upon them. It is all pride, all conceit, all self in some form. The aspects of it are countless. The Lord looks at it and says, "No, it is not of Christ; therefore, in the final issue it has to go!" That is why He breaks us, and empties us, and brings us down to the place where we cry from a deep, heart-broken consciousness: "Lord, unless Thou doest it, it is impossible! Unless Thou dost speak the word, my words are useless!" That is why He works in that way. The Lord in His sovereignty sees to it that we meet with plenty of things to keep us humble.

The Lord keeps us humble through the difficult people He sets around us, and whom He does not take away however much we cry to Him to do so, even though in themselves they are all wrong and an apparent menace to the Lord's interests. They serve to keep us humble and dependent. The Lord does that sort of thing, all in keeping with this law, that everything is us must be of Christ. Christ fills the universe for God. If He sees anything but what is of Christ, it cannot have a place. Only His Son can fill all things, excluding everything else. Oh, how humbly we need to seek of the Lord that there shall be nothing about us that, as of ourselves, presses itself upon others—our manner, our mannerisms, our presence, our conduct, our spirit, even our voice. The Spirit would oft-times check us and cause us to walk softly. None of us has attained to very high levels in this matter, and we are all having to acknowledge failure. The Spirit is dealing with us in that way. If even in our dress, or in any other thing, *we* come into view as the Lord's children, the Holy Spirit would seek to bring us to a place of sensitiveness, where He can say: "That is bringing yourself into view! That is out from you! Now, get covered, get hidden! That thing excludes Christ!"

God has determined from all eternity that this universe shall be filled with Christ, the Heavenly Man, through that corporate Heavenly Man joined to Him as its Head. He is getting rid of the Jew in us, of the Greek in us, and constituting us according to Christ, conforming us to the image of His Son. Blessed be God! The moment we come to the place where the last remnants and relics of what is not of Christ fall from us, then He will be displayed in us; He shall come to be glorified in the saints. It is Christ who is to be glorified, not ourselves; yet so close is the relationship that He is to be glorified in us. The Lord hasten the day!

SEVEN

THE HEAVENLY MAN
AS THE INSTRUMENT
OF THE GENERAL PURPOSE

The Heavenly Man personally is presented to us by the Apostle John in a fuller way than by any other of the New Testament writers. Paul advances to the corporate Heavenly Man. That does not mean that Paul does not present the personal Heavenly Man, for he undoubtedly does, particularly in his letter to the Colossians; but he advances from the personal Heavenly Man to the corporate Heavenly Man, which is the Church, His Body.

May we repeat one thing. Christ, actually and literally, was with the Father before times eternal, and the Church, not actually and literally, but in foreknowledge and foreordination, was also with the Father and the Son before times eternal. The fullest unveiling of the Church, which comes to us through the Apostle Paul, reveals it as already completed when Paul wrote. It was not finished numerically and it was anything but finished spiritually and morally, yet he speaks of it as though it were the most complete, the most perfect thing in the universe. He is standing, as it were, at God's side, and God views the Church from the eternal standpoint, that is, as outside of time.

THE RESTORATION OF HEAVENLY RELATIONSHIP

Recognising, then, that Christ and the Church are revealed as being with the Father from all eternity, we next see that by reason of that which has taken place in the fall, and which was anticipated in the redemptive line of purpose, Christ comes into time, and is born in time in relation to redemption, and that redemption is said to be from "this present evil age" (Galatians i. 4). The Authorised Version renders it "world," but the change is important. It is not from a place that we are redeemed, but from an age, and it is perfectly clear what that age is. It embraces all the intermediary sections or dispensations. The present evil age runs from Adam to the new heavens and the new earth. There is a coming glorious age. To be redeemed out of this present evil age, means that the Church, which belongs to eternity and not to this age, is to be redeemed out of it. It shows how Christ, by redemption, brings back into the straight line of what is eternal and outside of time, into the eternal counsels and purposes of God concerning His Son. By the redemption that is in Christ Jesus, which is a redemption from this evil age, the Church is redeemed unto that other age, that eternal age. So the birth of Christ is related to the redemption of the purchased possession, the redemption of the Church.

Coming to John, firstly with regard to Christ's entry into time, we find that John has three things to say about Christ.

(i) John sets Christ in eternity.

"In the beginning was the Word, and the Word was with God, and the Word was God" (John i. 1). That is Christ outside of time.

(ii) He shows Christ's coming into time.

"And the Word became flesh, and dwelt among us..." (John i. 14).

(iii) Christ is revealed as being also in Heaven while here.

This third thing which is stated in John's Gospel is declared by the Lord Himself, and combines both of the other two things. The Son, who is here in the flesh, is at the same time in heaven. There is the uniting of the two spheres. While He is here, He is still in heaven; while He is in time, He is still in eternity. "And no one hath ascended into heaven, but he that descended out of heaven, even the Son of man, who is in heaven" (John iii. 13). That is the Heavenly

Man as presented to us by John; Christ on earth, and at the same time still in heaven.

Now, in Christ, that becomes true of the Church, and is true of every member of the Church. In Christ we are here, and at the same time in heaven. We are in time, but we are also in eternity. The question arises, how can this be? It is a statement which needs explaining.

This brings us to the point where eternal and heavenly relationship is resumed. That relationship was broken off, interrupted. In Christ, as representative Man, it is resumed, taken up again. With Him it has never been interrupted. The interruption had to do with man, but through union with Christ that relationship—howbeit in a fuller way—is resumed, or restored to man. What is the point at which this resumption takes place? It is what is known amongst us as being born anew, or from above. Its law and its main spring is eternal life.

ISRAEL AND THE PROMISES

Two things were evidently related in the Jewish mind. These were (i) the kingdom of heaven, and (ii) eternal life. Nicodemus asked what he must do to enter the kingdom of heaven. Another ruler, probably of the same school as Nicodemus, and perhaps of the same rank, asked this question: "Teacher, what shall I do to inherit eternal life?" (Luke x. 25). These things were evidently accepted by the Jews as a promise. The Lord Jesus recognised and referred to that expectation when He said, "Ye search the scriptures, because ye think that in them ye have eternal life..." (John v. 39). There was a quest for eternal life, an expectation, a hope of eternal life, a persuasion that eternal life was a promise to be realised. These two things were linked together in their mind. Christ associates this hope with Himself and says concerning the testimony of the Scriptures, "...these are they which bear witness of *me*." To such as can receive it, He indicates that He Himself is the way or ladder into Heaven, the necessary means of getting there. We are, of course, referring to John i. 51. Now read verse 47:

"Jesus saw Nathanael coming to him, and saith of him,
Behold, an Israelite indeed, in whom is no guile!"

Here is a pure Israelite. What can you say to a pure Israelite who is looking for the kingdom of heaven and eternal life, a man who is true, a man who is honest? The Lord has seen him under the fig tree, really pouring himself out in quest of the kingdom of heaven and eternal life, if what the Lord Jesus said to him is a clue to what was going on in his heart. He was of those who looked for the blessings of Israel.

Let us pause for a moment, and insert Psalm cxxxiii here in brackets. "Behold, how good and how pleasant it is for brethren to dwell together in unity!...for there Jehovah commanded the blessing, even life for evermore." How does the blessing come? Whence is this hope, this expectation of the blessing? Our question takes us back to the promise made to Abraham: "...in thee shall all the families of the earth be blessed" (Genesis xii. 3). These Israelites were looking for the blessing of Abraham. But note what is further said: "...in Isaac shall thy seed be called" (Genesis xxi. 12). What does Isaac represent? Life from the dead, Divine life. The blessing of Abraham is life. Now note the words of the psalm: "...for there Jehovah commanded the blessing, even life for evermore." So you see that what they were in quest of was the blessing which had these two aspects, the kingdom of heaven, and eternal life.

In Nathanael we see an Israelite indeed in whom there is no guile, a pure man in a right quest. The Lord says to a man like that, "...Ye shall see the heaven opened, and the angels of God ascending and descending upon the Son of man." Are you in quest of the kingdom of heaven? "Ye shall see the heaven opened..." Are you wanting to get through? You will need a ladder, a way, a means, a vehicle: "Ye shall see...the angels of God ascending and descending upon the Son of man."

Nathanael knew exactly to what the Lord was referring. An Israelite indeed, in whom there was no guile, was Nathanael! Let us recall the incident to which the Lord referred. "And Jacob...lighted upon a certain place...And he took one of the stones of the place, and put it under his head, and lay down in that place to sleep. And he dreamed. And behold, a ladder set up on the earth, and the top of it reached to heaven. And behold, the angels of God ascending and descending on it. And, behold, Jehovah stood above it, and said…I am with thee, and will keep thee, whithersoever thou goest….And Jacob awaked out of his sleep, and he said…How dreadful is this place! This is none other but the house of God, and this is the gate of heaven" (Genesis xxviii. 10-17)—Bethel, the House of God: the House of God, the gate of heaven. The Lord Jesus appropriates that and says, in effect: "I am the House of God, I am the gate of heaven. Thou shalt see heaven open through Me." Do you want to know how to reach heaven? Two things have to be considered; one is the fact of union with Christ, the other is that which is bound up with union with Christ—namely, eternal life.

MAN BY NATURE AN OUTLAW

Let us stay with that for a moment. "Ye shall see the heaven opened…." Such a statement implies that the heavens have been closed. That, again, carries with it the fact that for man eternal life has also been put behind a closed heaven. Even for Nathanael, even for Nicodemus, even for a pure-hearted Israelite that is true by nature. Their longing is for an opened heaven. They are stretched out for the kingdom of heaven, but it is closed.

We know quite well that to everyone by nature, Heaven is a closed realm. But a closed Heaven is not God's thought for us. We belong to heaven. Christ belongs to heaven. The Church belongs to heaven. Yet the very place to which we belong is closed to us. The place with which we are related in the eternal counsels and purpose of God is closed to us by nature. That has its most terrible manifestation in those moments of the Cross, when the Lord Jesus, standing in the place of man in his sinful state, cried, "My God, my God why hast thou forsaken me?" Heaven is closed to Me; the place to which I belong, My heaven, My home, is closed to Me! I am an outcast from heaven!

Such is the state of man by nature, shut out from heaven, the place for which he was made, the place which belongs to him in the purpose of God. The Lord says to Nathanael, "Ye shall see the heaven opened." There is far more meaning in the phrase we so often use, "an open heaven," than we have recognised. What is it to enjoy an open heaven? It is to be at home in fellowship with the Lord; it is to have a heavenly life; it is to have all the heavenly resources at our disposal; all that Heaven means is open to us, and we have come into that for which God brought us into being, which he intended to be ours from all eternity; that is an opened heaven. "Ye shall see the heaven opened...." Then the quest of the heart is satisfied, the promise realised. The principle of the opened heaven, or of the heavenly life, is what is called eternal life in Christ. Christ is the Heavenly Man, coming into time.

CHRIST AND THE CHURCH

We have said once or twice that the Church is to be what the Heavenly Man was, and is, as to His being, as to the laws of His life, as to His ministry. Everything that is true about Him as the Heavenly Man has to become true of the Church. Thus, seen as the Lord Jesus, as the Heavenly Man, was born here in time, so also is the Church, the corporate Heavenly Man, to have a birth here in time, and on the same principle as Christ was born.

How was Christ born? You will realise that we are leaving the question of Deity on one side. We are not touching that side at all. In the sense in which Christ was God incarnate, Immanuel, God with us, God manifest in the flesh, that is not true of us as members of the Church. That is understood. We are talking about the Heavenly Man, not of the Divine Son, not of Godhead. So that what is true of Him as the Heavenly Man as to His birth, has to be true of the whole Church in every part. Let us look at the birth of the Lord Jesus and mark how it is characterised by three things.

(A) THE WORD PRESENTED

We go back to Luke, for Luke enlarges upon what John says. John compasses it all in one statement: "And the Word became flesh, and dwelt among us...." It is Luke who gives us the fullest description of the Word being made flesh, the birth of Christ. We will not read the whole story, but we mark first of all how that the angel went to Mary, and began to present Mary with a statement. He made his statement to her, and then waited. In her perplexity she asked a question. He answered her question, and again waited. Then came the response: "Behold, the handmaid of the Lord; be it unto me according to thy word" (Luke i. 38). First of all the word offered: that is the first step in His birth, the word presented, the statement made. Then the angel waited. What are you going to do with it? How are you going to react to it? The word presents a challenge, always a costly challenge. That word is going to lead outside of the world, and is to bring the liberty of the world. Mary weighs the cost while the angel waits. The battle is fought, the storm for a moment rages, and then it is over, and in calm deliberateness, she responds, "...be it unto me according to *thy word.*"

Do you see what it means to be begotten of the word of God? The first step in this new birth, the first step into this heavenly life, is our attitude toward the presented word of God, and that will be found to govern every step in the heavenly life. Such is the nature of the first step, and it is equally that of every subsequent step. All the way through the Lord will be presenting us with His word, and with it a challenge, a cost, a price to be paid, and there will be conflict over it: Are we prepared to go that way? Are we prepared to accept that word? Are we prepared for what that word means, for what it involves? On the response to what is presented depends our knowledge of the heavenly life. From beginning to end it is like that.

That is why the Lord never first explains everything to unsaved people. Doctrine followed for believers but was never given for unbelievers. Clear, concise statements were made to unbelievers. To them there was a presenting of facts, boldly and deliberately. "This is God's will. This is God's word. This you must do. Explanation will come later. Now, Heaven is going to remain closed, or is going to be opened; the question of your entry into a heavenly life hangs in the balance as you decide what is to be your response to God's word. You will be born of that word, if you respond to it, begotten by the word of truth." So the first thing is the word offered, and then, after some difficulty and conflict, accepted, received, surrendered to: "...be it unto me according to thy word."

(B) THE WORD GERMINATING

What is the next step? The Spirit makes the word to germinate within. The Spirit generates within by means of the word. That is the second thing to be noted in the case of Mary, the Spirit generating, or implanting. Not until the word has found a response can that word become a living thing within. That is why an unsaved person can never know the meaning of the Word of God. The meaning of any word of God demands the inward work of the Holy Spirit to make it live, to make it germinate, and response to it opens the way for the Spirit.

(C) THE WORD (CHRIST) FORMED WITHIN INITIALLY AND PROGRESSIVELY

That is the third step. It is very simple when presented like that, but this is the way into Heaven, into eternal life. Mark you, this is something other than of Mary, her race, and her nature. By the Holy Spirit there was a complete coming in between all that Mary was by nature and that Holy Thing. It is a very important matter, moreover, for us to recognise that in exactly the same way are we born anew. When Christ was born of Mary, or when Christ was (may we use the word?) generated in Mary, there took place in Mary something that was altogether above nature. Mary had a long natural lineage, and in that lineage there were all sorts of people, including several harlots. But when the Holy Spirit came in and formed Christ in her, He set all that aside and cut it off. That blood did not come into Christ. Remember that! He did not inherit aught of that, whatever it was, whether high or low, good or bad. The Holy Spirit cut it off, and Christ was something other than that, distinct: "…the holy thing…." You can never say that of anything that is inherited of the blood of Rahab, or of Ruth the Moabitess. It is something other.

Christ in us is something other than ourselves. That is what makes us heavenly. Flesh and blood cannot inherit the kingdom of Heaven. That is our natural stream, our natural history, the whole course of our Adamic relationship, which cannot inherit the kingdom of Heaven. It is only what is of Christ that will inherit the kingdom of Heaven. It is Christ in us who is to us the hope of glory, and the only hope of glory. This is something other than of Mary, and her race and nature, something other than of ourselves. This which is begotten of God is of the Holy Ghost. You and I ever need to discriminate between what is of Christ in us and what is of ourselves, and not to get these things mixed. Nothing that is not of Christ is going to find acceptance. Everything has to measure up to Christ, to pass through the sieve of Christ, and the sieve is a very fine one; for everything has to go through the test of death, and death is a tremendous test. Is there anything that death can lay hold of? If there is, it will lay hold of it. All that is subject to death will succumb to death, and this old creation is nothing else but that. Christ is not subject to death; He cannot be holden of it, for there is nothing in Him upon which death can fasten. That is our hope of glory, Christ in us. This Holy Ghost dividing between Mary and Christ, between ourselves and Christ, this fundamental division made by the Holy Ghost, must be kept constantly in mind, for only as we do that can God reach His end. Mark you, God can reach His end far more rapidly where that discrimination is maintained, than He can where it is overlooked. That is the importance of believers being instructed of the Lord concerning that which is essential unto His purpose.

Christ was other than the rest of men in that respect. Even from childhood He had another consciousness, as we have occasion to note when He is at the age of twelve. Not finding Him in their company, His earthly parents sought Him, and found Him in the temple, and claimed Him as son: "Son, why hast thou thus dealt with us? behold, thy father and I sought thee sorrowing." To this He replied, "...knew ye not that I must be in my Father's house?" (Luke ii. 48, 49). It is a reproof, but at the same time a disclosure of another consciousness. "Thy father and I..."—"...my Father's house...." That is not Joseph's house. Here is the setting of one Father over against the other, and of the one above the other. It is a heavenly consciousness, an eternal consciousness, a mark that He is "other," as begotten of the Holy Ghost.

When, begotten of the Holy Ghost, we come at once back into our eternal relationship with God in the Son, a new consciousness springs up within us, a consciousness that was not there before. This "new man" which has been put on, has a new consciousness as to heavenly relationships.

All that is embraced in the words "eternal life." We know that eternal life does not merely imply the fact of duration; it means a kind of life. That eternal life, that life from above, that Divine life in Christ, carries with it all that relates to the Heavenly Man.

Consider the Heavenly Man personally again. "In him was life..." (John i. 4); "For as the Father hath life in himself, even so gave he to the Son also to have life in himself..." (John v. 26). In the Gospel of John, the Lord Jesus says much about Himself as the Heavenly Man, possessing heavenly life, and that heavenly life was the seat of the heavenly nature and the heavenly consciousness; it was through that heavenly life that He conducted Himself as He did. He was alive unto God by that life which He possessed, and this is seen in His being able to know God, to know the movements of God, the directions of God, the gestures of God, the restraints of God. It was all gathered up in that life. That is the principle of His life as of His birth. It is the principle of our birth, and alike the principle of our life as the corporate Heavenly Man.

THE GIFT OF THE HOLY SPIRIT

That life is by the Holy Spirit. It is always related to a Person; it is not an abstract, a mere element. It is inseparable from the Person, which Person is the Holy Spirit; and the Holy Spirit is the Spirit of Jesus. When you come to the Book of the Acts, you have a great deal disclosed about the gift of the Holy Spirit. If you look at it closely you will see that the coming of the Holy Spirit was invariably related to spiritual union with Christ. Pentecost marked the end of a physical relationship with the Lord Jesus as in the flesh, the end of that extraordinary period of His post-resurrection appearances. It is the beginning of an inward, spiritual relationship with Christ. We may mark the same feature at Caesarea; they believed, and the Holy Spirit was given. At Samaria, again, hands were laid upon those who had believed, and the Holy Spirit was given. And one of the most interesting things in the Book of the Acts is that incident at Ephesus.

When Paul came to Ephesus, he found certain disciples, and discerned something unusual in their condition, or was it something lacking? To them he says, "Did ye receive the Holy Spirit when ye believed?" (Acts xix. 2). That is the correct translation, not "since ye believed" as in the King James Version. That in itself assumes that believing implies the receiving of the Spirit. The two things go together. Paul could not quite understand this situation. It was something abnormal. Here were those who professed to believe in Christ, and who in a way had believed in Christ, but that which should go alongside of true faith was not there. Paul found himself confronted by a condition he had never met with before, and on his putting them to the question, "Did ye receive the Holy Spirit when ye believed?" they made answer, "Nay, we did not so much as hear whether the Holy Spirit was...." So Paul further enquires, "Into what then were ye baptized?" to which they replied, "Into John's baptism." Ah! now we have the clue. "John baptized with the baptism of repentance, saying unto the people that they should believe on him that should come after him, that is, on Jesus." So they had been baptised into John's baptism, unto an objective, future Christ; not baptised into Christ, but baptised toward Christ. Those are two different baptisms altogether. Paul commanded them to be baptised into the Name of the Lord Jesus, laid his hands upon them, and the Holy Ghost was given. Those two things go together. Union with Christ is shown to involve the receiving of the Spirit. That is not intended by the Lord to be something later on in the spiritual life; it should mark the commencement.

If in the Book of the Acts there are particular elements which throw up the whole matter into such clear relief, such as accompanying signs, those signs were only the Lord's way of emphasising for all the dispensation what it means, that union with Christ involves the receiving of the Holy Spirit. How do you know? Well, He has shown it to this dispensation by bringing it out into clear relief in that way. He has laid it down so that no one can fail to see it. If you become occupied with the signs (tongues, etc.), but miss their signification, you will fail to see that those outward marks, those demonstrations, were only allowed as accompaniments, in order to emphasise the basic truth, namely, that union with Christ was now established. The gift of the Holy Spirit was the seal and proof of this. On what ground? By believing in Christ, by being baptized into Christ, eternal life is received in the Holy Spirit. And that life has heavenly capacities, within it are the powers of the age to come; and when in the ages to come its powers are fully released, we shall be endued with powers which far transcend our present powers. The age to come has been foreshadowed in tokens at the beginning. It may be that from time to time those powers are made manifest in the healing of the sick even now, but let us not fasten upon those tokens and make a doctrine of tokens and signs, begin to gather them up and systematise them, and make them the object of our quest. Let us remember that they are the tokens of something else, and you can have the "something else" apart from the tokens. When in truth you are baptised into Christ, you receive the Spirit of life in Christ, and in that life you are at once brought back into your heavenly relationship with the Heavenly Man; you become part of the corporate Heavenly Man.

It is what Christ is in us by His Spirit that determines everything. It determines all the values, settles for ever the question of effectiveness, answers all the questions and problems. I wish we had had this understanding, this knowledge sooner. If only we could have this as the foundation of our life from the beginning, what a lot we should be saved from.

Ministry is the expression of life, and not the taking on of a uniform and a title. Once I thought that to be in the ministry was to go into a certain kind of work, to come out of business, and, well, be a minister! So one got into the thing. Many, many are labouring and toiling in it, breaking their hearts, afraid to leave that order of things, lest they should be violating what they conceived to be a Divine call. Many others cannot get out of it because it is a means of livelihood, and they too are breaking their hearts. It is all false. Ministry is not a system like that. Ministry is the expression of life, and that is but saying in other words that it is the outworking of the indwelling of Christ. Disaster lies before the man or woman who ministers on any other ground than that. When the Lord gets a chance in us, and we really will trust Him on that ground, take our position there, He will show us that there is ministry enough for us; we shall not have to go round looking for it. The real labour so often is to get us down to that ground, the delivering of us from this present evil age even in its conception of the ministry, unto the heavenly ministry.

The Lord Jesus is our pattern. You see the spontaneous ministry, the restful ministry of that Heavenly Man. I covet that! It does not mean that we shall become careless, but it does deliver us from so much unnecessary strain. That is how it should be. May the Lord bring us to it; the Heavenly Man with the heavenly life as the full heavenly resource.

EIGHT

THE HEAVENLY MAN
AS THE SOURCE AND
SPHERE OF CORPORATE UNITY

Reading: Ephesians iv. 1-16, 30-32; Psalm cxxxiii.

Here we have a psalm which, on the one hand, presents an imperfect or partial entering into the spirit of the blessing of which it speaks, and, on the other hand, a prophecy; a type and prophecy of the full blessing to come, and a present but imperfect enjoyment of the meaning of the blessing. As a type of prophecy of the full blessing to come, it indicates the basis of the blessing, and the wonderful beneficent elements of the blessing. Read the Psalm backward and you will at once see what the basis is: "...there Jehovah commanded the blessing, even life for evermore." Where was the blessing given? "Behold, how good and how pleasant it is for brethren to dwell together in unity!"—"...there Jehovah commanded the blessing, even life for evermore." Between the first and the last verses the beneficent influence and effect of the blessing is seen, which blessing is based upon two things. One of these is brought to our notice in the preceding psalm. You will recognize that these are "Psalms of Ascents." That, again, speaks of the partial enjoyment of the meaning of the blessing. The people are going up to Zion; they are in caravan, in procession, coming up from the distant parts with their eyes and their hearts all toward Zion in expectation, in hope; Zion the city of their solemnities; Zion the joy of all the earth; Zion the unifying centre of all their life; Zion in the ways of which they were but which was also in their hearts as a way—"...in whose heart are the highways to Zion" (Psalm lxxxiv. 5).

THE UNIFYING CENTRE

Now you see Zion is there as a great unifying factor. People from all directions are coming in procession. Some have joined the caravan at various places as it has moved on from its most distant point, and they find that although they may never have met before on earth; although they may only just have come into touch with one another for the first time in their lives; although their paths may lie far apart in ordinary life, their sphere of life and service be divided and separate, Zion makes them a unity. Immediately the thoughts of Zion are in their hearts, immediately they think of Zion and move toward Zion, all scatteredness, separateness, divisiveness passes out, and they are as one man. Zion has unified them.

Now let us mark what is brought before us in Psalm cxxxii:

*"Surely I will not come into the tabernacle of **my** house,*
*nor go up into **my** bed; I will not give sleep to **mine** eyes,*
*or slumber to **mine** eyelids; until I find out a place for*
Jehovah, a tabernacle for the Mighty One of
Jacob....Arise, O Jehovah, into thy resting-place; thou,
and the ark of thy strength....This is my resting-place for
ever: here will I dwell; for I have desired it. I will abun-
dantly bless her provision: I will satisfy her poor with
bread" (Psalm cxxxii. 3-5, 8, 14-15).

The first factor in the basis of the blessing is God's satisfaction, God finding His satisfaction: "Arise, O Jehovah, into thy resting-place...." Here we have the Lord coming to rest in His House. This is not to be interpreted mentally in a literal way. It is a case of the Lord having a ground of perfect satisfaction, the Lord having things according to His own mind, His own heart, the Lord just finding what He has been seeking all the time: "This is my resting-place for ever...." The Lord has been provided with that which answers to His own heart's desire, and it is therefore possible to say to Him, "Arise, O Jehovah, into thy resting-place...."

David's concern was that the Lord should be satisfied first of all. You will notice from the passage we have quoted that he sets aside all that is his own. With David, the Lord takes first place.

CHRIST—GOD'S ALL AND OURS

Let us carry that over to the New Testament for interpretation, for it is there that we shall find the spiritual meaning. We are meditating upon "*all things in Christ*," and amongst these things, and by no means least, is God's satisfaction, God's coming to rest in His Tabernacle. That is what was in point when the Spirit, descending in the form of a dove, lighted upon the Lord Jesus. The dove returning to her rest in the Ark typified the Spirit coming to rest in Christ, the satisfaction of God: "This is my beloved Son, in whom I am well pleased" (Matthew iii. 17). "I find My rest, I am perfectly satisfied, here I have all My desire." So the Spirit as a dove, the symbol of peace and rest, lighted upon Him. The Lord Jesus answers to all the desire of God's heart, and in Him God enters into His rest.

When you and I set aside all our interests, and focus and concentrate all our concern upon the Lord Jesus, so that He has first place, has all, we have provided God with His rest in our lives, thus paving the way for the blessing. "There Jehovah commanded the blessing...." Where? Firstly, where He found His rest, His satisfaction, His joy. The Lord does not bless you and me as our natural selves. The Lord will not bless my flesh, nor your flesh. The blessing of the Lord comes to rest upon His Son as within us: "...the anointing which ye received of him abideth in you..." (I John ii. 27). Remember that the blessing of the Lord, the anointing, the precious ointment, is upon the Head. It comes down to us only as from the Head, by way of the Head, and it is when Christ by His Spirit has come to rest in us that the blessing rests there. The blessing rests upon Him in us, and that is why it abides. Thank God, it abides. This, if we do but recognise it, is one of the chief blessings of our life in union with the Lord. We in ourselves do not abide for five minutes! We can be as changeable as the weather. In the morning we may be one man, and in the afternoon another, and in the evening quite another. We may be as many different people in the course of the week as there are days. At one time we feel splendid spiritually and think we shall never, never be down again, but it is not long before we are right down. We vary like that; we become familiar with every movement that this human life is capable of knowing. If we live in that soul-life of constantly changing moods, oh, what a distressing life it is. But the anointing which you have received abideth. Why is this? Because it abides upon Him, not upon us, and He is "the same yesterday and to-day, yea and for ever" (Hebrews xiii. 8). There is no changing on the part of the Lord Jesus in us. With Him, there is no variableness, neither shadow cast by turning. Oh, the changes that sweep over our lives because of the changeableness of this human life; but there He is in us ever the same. We may have a thousand moods in as many hours, but He never changes, He is always the same. The anointing abides upon Him in us. Oh, that we should live in Christ, live in the anointing, live in that unvarying fact of God in Christ, unchangeable. He does not love us in the morning and turn against us in the afternoon. However we may feel it to be so, such is not the case. "I have loved thee with an everlasting love" (Jeremiah xxxi. 3). Our moods would lead us to conclude that to-day the Lord loves us, and to-morrow that He is against us; to-day that the Lord is with us, to-morrow that He has departed from us. That is our infirmity. That is of ourselves and not of the Lord. The Lord is not us, in that way. The Lord is not our moods, our feelings, our sensations, or our lack of sensations. The Lord is the same always, the same faithful, unchangeable God, and the anointing abideth. It does not come and go. It does not rise and fall. It is not in and out, up and down, one day this and the next day that; it abides.

The enjoyment of that is only possible when Christ is the focal point of our lives. God comes to rest in His Son, and finds His satisfaction there. You must come there in order to find God's rest, and then the blessing is there. The Lord commands the blessing in the place where He has His rest, that is, in the Lord Jesus. But then Christ is in you: "...thou, and the ark of thy strength." That is Christ in you, the hope of glory.

CHRIST AS GOD'S REST IN THE HEART

So then, the first aspect of the basis of the blessing is that of our knowing God's rest in His Son, Jesus Christ, in our own lives. He

Himself put it in language which had to be more or less symbolic, or parabolic. "Take my yoke upon you, and learn of me; for I am meek and lowly in heart: and ye shall find rest unto your souls" (Matthew xi. 29). "Come unto me, all ye that labour and are heavy laden, and I will give you rest" (verse 28). We know what that means in the spirit. When we were children we may have thought it to be a word for labouring men in life's labours and toil, but we have come to know that this labouring and being heavy laden has mainly to do with these changeable moods of ours. We are labouring against the current, the tide, the stress of our own instability, our own uncertainty, our own oft-doubting and questioning, our feelings: and it is a labour when you live in that realm! The Lord Jesus says, "…I will give you rest." How will He do this? Well, He will come into you, take up His abode in you as the seat and centre of the deepest satisfaction, and you need have no more question. Are you straining and struggling over the question of whether the Lord is satisfied with you? You had better cease from it, because He never will be. If you are looking and longing for that day when the Lord is going to be perfectly satisfied with you, you are looking for a very distant day. If you are hoping that some day the Lord will be very pleased with you, and then you will be very happy, that day is not coming this side of glory. What we have to realise—and it is a truth so often repeated, and yet not grasped enough by our hearts—is that the Lord is never going to be satisfied with us as in ourselves, but He is already perfectly satisfied with His Son whom He has given to dwell in our hearts as the seat of His satisfaction, and we are accepted in the Beloved. Then the blessing comes. We see how the blessing works out.

DWELLING TOGETHER IN UNITY

Now we come to the second aspect of the basis of the blessing. *"Behold, how good and how pleasant it is for brethren to dwell together in unity!" (Psalm cxxxiii. 1).*

We have seen it in the illustration, the foreshadowing, namely, of Zion uniting all hearts, making all one, drawing away from everything personal, everything sectional. Now when the heart is centred upon the Lord Jesus, we have the greatest power and dynamic against division, against separateness, against everything that keeps us apart, and when the Lord Jesus is our central, supreme object, and it is toward Him that our hearts go out, then we come into a unity. You cannot have personal interests and at the same time care for the interests of the Lord. David makes that perfectly clear. "The tabernacle of *my* house," that is one thing; and if I consider that, then I shall not be set upon a house for the Lord; if I am set upon that, then I shall not find a place for the Lord's rest. If I am seeking to satisfy *my* desire, giving sleep to *my* eyes, and slumber to *my* eyelids, then the Lord's interests will take a second place. But when I set myself aside, with all that is personal, and I am centred upon the Lord, and when all the others do that too, we shall find our perfect uniting centre in Christ. That is what it is to dwell in unity.

Now Ephesians iv is the great New Testament exposition of Psalm cxxxii: "*There is* one body...." Read the passage without the italicised words: "...giving diligence to keep the unity of the Spirit in the bond of peace...one body, and one Spirit...one Lord, one faith, one baptism, one God and Father of all, who is over all, and through all, and in all" (verses 3-6). Oneness in Christ as a body fitly framed together is what is portrayed. How is this perfect unity reached? By all that is individual and personal being left, by the Lord being the focal centre, and by our giving diligence to maintain the unity in that way; keeping all personal things out, and keeping Christ and His interests always in view: "...till we all attain unto the unity of the faith, and of the knowledge of the Son of God, unto a fullgrown man..." (verse 13). Dwelling together in unity in that way, is the result of His being the sole and central object of all our concerns. This is not visionary, imaginative, merely idealistic, it is very practical. You and I will discover that there are working elements of divisiveness, things creeping in amongst us to set us apart. The enemy is always seeking to do that, and the things that rise up to get in between the Lord's people and put up a barrier are countless; a sense of strain and of distance, for example, of discord and of unrelatedness. Sometimes they are more of an abstract character; that is, you can never lay your hand upon them and explain them, and say what they are; it is just a sense of something. Sometimes it is more positive, a distinct and definite misunderstanding, a misinterpretation of something said or done, something laid hold of; and of course, it is always exaggerated by the enemy.

How is that kind of thing to be dealt with in order to keep the unity of the Spirit? Rightly, adequately on this basis alone, by our saying, "This is not to the Lord's interests; this can never be of value to the Lord; this can never be to His glory and satisfaction; this can only mean injury to the Lord." What I may feel in the matter is not the vital consideration. I may even be the wronged party, but am I going to feel wronged and hurt? Am I going to stand on my dignity? Am I going to shut myself up and go away, because I have been wronged? That is how nature would have it, but I must take this attitude: "The Lord stands to lose, the Lord's Name stands to suffer, the Lord's interests are involved in this; I must get on top of this; I must get the better of this; I must shake this thing off and not allow it to affect my attitude, my conduct, my feelings towards this brother or sister!" There must be the putting aside of that which we feel, and even of our rights for the Lord's sake, and a getting on top of this enemy effort to injure the Lord's testimony. That is giving diligence to keep the unity. That is the power of a victory over divisiveness, and is the victory for unity, and *there* the Lord commands the blessing. That is the way of eternal life. The other way is manifestly the way of death, and that is what the enemy is after. Until that difference is cleared up, all is death, all is withered and blighted. Life is by unity, and unity can only adequately be found in Christ being in His place as the One for whom we let go everything that is personal. We might not do it for the sake of anyone else. We might never do it for the sake of the person in view. We do it for His sake, and the enemy is defeated. There the Lord commands the blessing.

Such, then, is the twofold aspect of the basis of the blessing. Firstly, God's ground of satisfaction and rest must be equally our own, namely, His Son; and, secondly, we must dwell together therein.

Take the great illustration in the second chapter of the Book of the Acts. Here is the greatest exhibition of the working of this truth that the world has ever seen. "But Peter, standing up *with* the eleven...." There are brethren together in unity! The Lord also has

entered into His rest. By the Cross the Father has found His satisfaction in the Son; the Lord has entered into His heavenly Tabernacle. All is rest now in Heaven: God is satisfied, the reconciling work
has been done in the Blood of the Cross, peace has been made, and
God has entered into His rest in the perfect work of redemption. Now
the eyes of all the apostles are on the Lord Jesus, and as they stand
up He is in full view. Peter has left all those personal things behind.
They have all left the personal things now, and their whole object is
Christ. Standing up now, their testimony is all to Christ, and they are
one, united in Him; and there the Lord commanded the blessing,
even life for evermore, such blessing as was like the precious ointment coming down from the head to the skirts of the garment.

The figure is perfect, as a figure. There is the Head, the Lord
Jesus, and the Father has commanded the blessing in the pouring of
the eternal Spirit upon the Head. Now as all these members are
ranged under the Head, centred in the Head, held together in the
Head, the blessing comes down to the skirts of His garment, and it is
"like the dew of Hermon, that cometh down upon the mountains of
Zion...." That is the effect of the blessing, that is the effect of life for
evermore. What is the dew of Hermon? If you had lived in that country, you would know the value of the dew of Hermon. It is a parched
and shriveled land, with everything dry and becoming barren, and
then the dew of Hermon comes down and everything revives, everything is refreshed, everything lifts up its head and lives again. It is
the beneficent result of the blessing; life, freshness, hope, reviving,
fruitfulness. There the Lord commanded the blessing.

Do you see the way of life, the way of fruitfulness, of reviving,
of refreshing, the way of blessing? Two things are basic. These are
our coming to the place of God's rest in His Son, and our letting go
of everything that is of ourselves in the interests of His Son, and
finding our all in Him. Thus are we drawn together by our mutual
love for the Lord. Oh that we had more of the expression of this. I
think that is why the Lord is bringing the matter before us; not for
the message to be merely as a blessed prospect, a word that has a
happy ring about it and that gives us a certain amount of uplift while
it is being spoken, but for it to be a strong call from the Lord. Do we

want the blessing? Do we want life for evermore, life more abundant? Do we want refreshing, and fruitfulness, and reviving, and uplift? Do we want that others also should get the blessing through us? Look at Pentecost. Pentecost is the outworking of Psalm cxxxiii; for there brethren were dwelling together in unity, centred upon the Lord, and in the Lord, and the Lord commanded the blessing.

There is nothing very profound in this, but it is of no less importance on that account. It is yet another way of bringing the Lord Jesus into view, of showing Him as the centre, as supreme. But, oh, it is a call from the Lord, a serious and solemn call from the Lord to our hearts. The way of fruitfulness, the way of blessing, the way of freshness, the way of joy is to be in this way that is under the blessing of the Lord, because we have found our rest where He has found His, in the Lord Jesus; because the object of our hearts, for which we have set aside all lesser objects, all personal interests, is the object of His own, even His Son, our Lord Jesus Christ. There the Lord commands the blessing, even life for evermore.

May He be able to do that with us. Oh, that it might be said in days to come as never hitherto: "...*there* Jehovah commanded the blessing, even life for evermore," because of these two great governing realities, both of which are centred in the Lord Jesus.

NINE

THE HEAVENLY MAN AND ETERNAL LIFE

It is Christ as the Heavenly Man that is our consideration at this time, and we have been seeing that the main spring of the being of the Heavenly Man is eternal life. "In him was life..." (John i. 4); "For as the Father hath life in himself, even so gave he to the Son also to have life in himself" (John v. 26). It is eternal life, Divine life, life from God, a special kind of life; not merely extensiveness of life, but a nature of life. The main spring of His being as the Heavenly Man is eternal life. The Lord Jesus, as the Son of God, was ever appointed to be the Life-giver. From eternity that life was in Him for creation.

ETERNAL LIFE IN VIEW FROM ETERNITY

The words in the Gospel of John, used by the Lord Jesus, that it was given to Him of the Father both to have life in Himself, and to give that life unto whomsoever He willed, carry us back again into the "before times eternal." Here they relate to redemption, but that is not where the matter of life-giving, of God's intention with regard to life begins. We are shown in a figurative way that right at the beginning, before there was any fall, and therefore before there was any practical necessity for redemption, God's thought was eternal life, and when from fallen man He shut off the tree of life, He is seen to do so on this ground: "...lest he put forth his hand, and take also of the tree of life, and eat, and life for ever..." (Genesis iii. 22). Now God had made that provision. Eternal life was there in the thought and intention of God, but this eternal life was for a certain kind of man, and the Adam that came to be, as separated from God, ceased to stand in God's view as the being in whom eternal life could reside, and so that was reserved. It was maintained in the Son; for the tree surely is but a figure of Christ. When we get to the end of the Scripture the tree is seen again. Christ is the "tree of life." Christ is the repository of that life, and here He comes forth in man-form as the last Adam, as the kind of man in whom that life can be.

Through union with Him now by redemption, that life that is in Him is deposited in the believer himself; not as apart from Christ, but in Christ in the believer. It never departs from Christ. The Apostle states that this life is in His Son, and was given to us. We have eternal life, and this life is in His Son. It is Christ resident within in the person of His Spirit in whom the life is, and it is never possessed apart from Him.

We have been saying that the Lord Jesus, as the Son of God, was ever the appointed Life-giver. Of course, He can only so be known as Redeemer. He could have been known as the Life-giver apart from redemption, but now on account of man's condition through the fall, He can only be known as the Life-giver according as He is known as Redeemer. So that what we have to do with now, here in time, is redemption and life, redemption unto life.

REDEMPTION RELATED TO THE ETERNAL PURPOSE

Here we want again to speak for a few moments of that main line of eternal purpose which the Lord is seeking to bring us to, and to bring to us. Because it is so great, and lifts us so much out of that with which we are more entirely occupied in time, that is, our salvation, our redemption, and all that is associated with it; because it takes us out of that and puts us into so much larger a realm, it is quite natural that we should have difficulties and not be able to grasp it immediately. That is how we are finding it, and that is what is making necessary a return to this main emphasis.

Look again intently at the word "redemption." The word itself carries an implication. Redemption implies a bringing back. The question immediately presents itself: Brought back to what? And to what place? There is something that, for the time being, has been lost. It has ceased to remain in its original relationship, in its original position. It has to be brought back, reclaimed, restored, redeemed. Then there must have been a place and a position, and that is our main point.

We are seeking to say at this time, that before ever there was a fall, and even before this creation was, there was a counsel of God issuing in a purpose, and the straight line of that purpose through the ages was intended to work out progressively to a universal display of God in man, through His Son. So, through the Son, He created all things. Everything that was created in Heaven and in earth, and in the universe came, through the Son, to be "Son-wise" itself, God expressed and manifested in terms of "Son." In relation to that, we were "...foreordained...unto adoption as sons..." (Ephesians i. 5).

If you read the Word carefully you will descry Adam in the condition of a child, rather than of a son; a child under probation, under test; and because he failed under the test, he never came to the maturity of a son. Some of us are familiar with the New Testament teaching on the difference between a child of God and a son. Adam is in the infancy of God's thought, God's intention. He has to grow, to develop, to expand, to mature, to come to full stature; and we are not saying that the one test was the only one, the final test unto his maturity, but it was the first one. The whole plan of growth, of progressive development unto a full-grown, corporate man, does not necessarily rest upon redemption. It rests upon the eternal purpose, the eternal counsels. The straight line of things would have gone right on apart from any redemptive plan at all, and would have been realised. If Adam had not fallen, the eternal purpose would still have been realised, because it is all eternally vested in the Son. Now inasmuch as man is included, Adam was included. Adam failed and, with him, the race. Then a redemptive plan must come in; just as complete a plan in the counsels of God, but one developed or projected because of something that went wrong. We cannot say the fall was right, but it occasioned a plan, a perfect plan, a wonderful plan, and when God made the plan, when in His eternal counsels He was projecting this whole scheme of creation and intention and purpose, then the attitude, as we read back into those counsels, was undoubtedly this: "We know, because We cannot help knowing, being what We are, all-knowing, how things will go. We know that Our first thought will not be immediately realised, that there will be this bend down, this break. We therefore project this further plan of redemption by which We come down into that bend and bring things right up again on to Our level. We fill it up; but in so doing We will not lose. We will gain. This work of the adversary, all this tragedy, this suffering shall not take from Our original plan and thought, shall not diminish it one whit, neither shall it just mean that in the end We come back to Our level; We will come back with added glories, and these will be the glories of grace." God always reacts to the work of the Devil in that way; to get more than He had before, through suffering. Suffering is not God's will any more than sin is God's will, but in the sufferings of His own people He always secures something more than was there before. It is not only that He keeps even with the Devil, God is always "more than conqueror." That means that He obtains added glories as the result of the interference of His enemy, whatever may be said of that. This is so in the details of the individual experience, but in its fulness, in its whole movement, that interference occasioned the whole redemptive system and plan.

We recognise that, but that is not at the moment the thing with which we are dealing. Were it so, we should be speaking on the glories of redemption. But the Lord has laid this burden of His eternal thought for man upon our hearts at this time, and we do not believe that for one moment we are taking away from the glories of redemption, or putting redemption into a place of less value than it should have. If it seems to you that we are brushing that aside, or putting it into a secondary place, it is not that we are seeing less value in it than there is. God forbid! How are we to know God at all apart from it? At the same time, what we have in view is God's Son. It is not redemption, but the Son of God, this Heavenly Man, as representing God's full thought for man, and for the universe, with which we are dealing. The Son of God as Redeemer is but one expression of the Son, and one which, while so full of glory, and ever to be the theme of the redeemed through the ages of the ages, has become painfully necessary here in time. It speaks of tragedy. It speaks of Divine heart-break, of God suffering. This, however, as we have said, is not our main consideration at the present time, but in these meditations we are occupied with Christ as the Heavenly Man.

THE LOST TREASURE

We have said that we can only know Him as the Life-giver now in terms of redemption, as the Redeemer: "...the Son of man came to seek and to save that which was lost" (Luke xix. 10). What do we understand by that Scripture? Of course, in Gospel terms we have painted pictures of lost sheep, and we have thought of the individuals who are out and away from the Lord, as that which is lost. Well, that is quite true, but you have to be far more comprehensive than that in interpreting the Scripture. God has lost something, and the Son of Man has come to recover that which God has lost. What is it that God has lost? Listen again: "The kingdom of heaven is like unto a treasure hidden in the field; which a man found, and hid; and in his joy he goeth and selleth all that he hath, and buyeth that field" (Matthew xiii. 44). What is the treasure? What is the field? The field is the world, the treasure is the Church. That treasure is hid, and the Lord Jesus paid the price for the crown rights of the whole creation in order to have the Church which was in it. Christ acquired by redemption, by paying the price, universal rights in order to secure that treasure, the Church. This was it that was lost. What is the Church? The Church is the one new man, the fulness of the measure of the stature of a man in Christ. It is the corporate Heavenly Man, the expression of Himself in corporate form, His inheritance in the saints. That is a very precious treasure.

The Church is not the only thing, but it is the central thing. The Lord Jesus has acquired the rights of the universe, and there will be other things in addition to the Church. There will be the nations walking in the light thereof. There will be a redemption that goes far beyond the Church, but the Church is the central thing. He has found that, and it was this lost treasure that dictated His course, and governed Him in paying the price. That is a tremendous thought. The Church is so precious to Him as to make Him willing to pay the price for the whole universe, in order to have it. That is the focal point. The Church is the key to redemption. It is that which is coming to the perfect image of Christ. All else will be secondary. There will be a reflection of Christ through the Church; His light will fall upon all else; what He is will come to rest upon all else; all else will take its character from what He is in the Church, but the Church will be at the centre: "And the nations shall walk amidst the light thereof..." (Revelation xxi. 24). It is a tremendous thing to live in this dispensation when the Lord, though having acquired the rights of the universe, of the whole creation, by His Cross, is specifically concentrated upon the treasure now, to get it out of the creation.

"The kingdom of heaven [it should be in the plural, the kingdom of the heavens] is like unto a treasure hidden in the field; which a man found, and hid...." The Lord is doing a secret work in relation to the Church. It is always a dangerous thing to bring what we conceive to be the Church out into a conspicuous place, and make a public thing of it. The real Church is a secret, hidden company, and a hidden and secret work is going on in it. That is its safety. When you and I launch out into great public movements, displaying and advertising, we expose the work of God, and open it to infinite perils. Our safety is in keeping where God has put us, in the hidden, secret place with Himself. That by the way.

"The kingdom of heaven [the heavens] is like unto...." What is the significance of that phrase? It means that the whole heavenly system is focused upon the Church. It is the centre of the heavenly system. All that "the heavens" means, in this spiritual sense, is interested in the Church, is concerned with the Church, the treasure in the field. Why is this? Because, again, the Church is the *Heavenly* Man in Christ.

Take the Lord Jesus in person, as the Heavenly Man. The whole universe is interested in Him. At His birth Heaven is active; the hosts of heavenly beings break through in relation to Him. Hell also is active and, through Herod, seeks to destroy this birth and all its meaning. You find that right on through His earthly life all the universe is centring its attention upon Him, and is related to Him, so that in His death the sun hides its face, the earth quakes, and there is darkness over the face of it. The whole universe is bound up with this One.

Thus the kingdom of the heavens, all the heavenly system, is concerned with this treasure in the field, because of its eternal significance, relationship, purpose. This is an immense thing. Now, of course, you are able to appraise more perfectly the value and meaning of redemption. To see the background of things is not to take away from redemption, it is to add marvelously to it. It is to give to redemption a meaning far removed from that of just being saved as a unit here and getting to Heaven. That is a big thing, of course, that saving of the individual. But when we see the redemption that is in Christ Jesus in the light of God's eternal background, how immense a thing it is! If you want really to appreciate, and rightly appraise redemption, you have to set it where Paul set it, and see that it is cosmic. The coming into redemption on the part of every single individual is a coming into something immense, a far bigger thing than the redemption of the individual himself. All the powers and intelligences of the universe are bound up with, and interested in, this redemption. We believe that in order rightly to appreciate and enjoy the things of God, it is necessary to get their universal and eternal background, and not take them as something in themselves. That is how Paul saw redemption.

ETERNAL LIFE THE VITAL PRINCIPLE OF REDEMPTION

The vital principle in redemption has to be implanted. Redemption is not something objective, something that is done for us. It is that, but it is not just that. It is not merely a system carried through, but redemption embraces a vital principle which has to become implanted in the believer, and the vital principle in redemption is eternal life, the life of the ages. So that redemption, bringing with it its vital principle, at once swings us back into relation with Christ before times eternal as the appointed Life-giver, and then we are carried right through with deathless life. Redemption itself, by itself, that principle of eternal life, expresses itself in the bringing back to the place where God can do what He found it impossible to do with the first Adam, to the place where He can give eternal life. When we come into redemption, all the ages of this world are wiped out as a matter of time, and we find ourselves at once made eternal beings, linked back there with the timeless God. The vital principle of redemption is eternal life to be implanted in the redeemed.

REDEMPTION PROGRESSIVE IN THE BELIEVER BY THE LIFE PRINCIPLE

The next thing, working out from that, is that this vital principle of redemption makes the perfect redemption which is in Christ Jesus progressive in us. In Christ our redemption is perfect. We have a full redemption in Christ. His being in glory betokens that redemption is complete, full and final. But when the vital principle of redemption, that is, eternal life, is introduced into us through faith, this, which is perfect in Christ as redemption, takes up a progressive course in us as that principle of life. Redemption becomes progressive in us

by life. That life is a progressive thing. We only come to the understanding and the enjoyment of the full redemption as the life increases in us. It is the work of redemption life in us which is going to
bring us to the fulness of redemption. That is going to be proved true
in spirit, mind, and body. We are going to enter into the fulness of
redemption that is in Christ's present heavenly, physical body. His body,
His present heavenly physical body, is a representation, a standard of the
redemption of our complete humanity. We are going to be made like
unto His glorious body. By what principle is this to be accomplished? By the working of that redemption life in us progressively.

THE TWOFOLD LAW OF THE LIFE

Now, how does that redemption life in us operate? It operates in
two ways. On the one hand, it operates to cut us off from our own
natural life as the basis of our relationship with God. That is a big
thing, and a big work, and a very deep work. So many in spiritual
infancy and immaturity are making their own natural life, energies,
resources, enthusiasms, and all such things, the basis of their relationship with the Lord both in life and service. It is a mark of immaturity. We know quite well that the young believer is always full of
tremendous enthusiasm, and thinks it to be the real strength of his
union with God, and that it really does represent something in relation to God. When presently the March winds begin to blow, and the
blossom is carried away, such as these think the Winter has come
instead of the Summer. They think they have lost everything. They
ask, "What has happened to me?" The words of the hymn are perhaps
heard upon their lips:

> *"Where is the blessedness I knew*
> *When first I saw the Lord?"*

But you do not get the fruit until the blossom has gone. It is the
Summer, not the Winter, that follows the blowing away of the blossom. Of course, we all like to see the blossom in its time, but we
should have some strange feelings if we saw the blossom there all
through the Summer. We should say: "There is something wrong
here, it is time that blossom went." We look closer, and we see something in its place, full of promise, and of much more value. This

early blossom may be a sign of life, but it is not the life itself. A sign of early life belongs to the early Spring, showing that the Winter is past and resurrection is at work. It is a sign but it is not the thing itself, and it passes with spiritual infancy. These early enthusiasms are not the real basis of our union with God, but are signs of something that has happened in us. They are of ourselves, they are not of God. He is something other than that. He is not going to blow away. The life is working and will show itself in stronger and deeper forms.

All the way through this life we have to learn the change from what is, after all, ourselves in relation to God, to what is God Himself in us. There is a great deal that is of ourselves in relation to God, and I expect there will be in some measure right to the end. There is still something of our minds at work on God's things. We may be thinking that they are God's thoughts, God's mentality, but there is still much that is of our human mind, the mental make-up of ourselves in relation to the things of God, and we shall always find that God's mind is other than that, and we have to give place to new conceptions of the Lord. In will and in heart it is just the same.

We have been speaking of the body. This law of life works to the removing of our natural basis in relation to the Lord, so that even in our physical being we come on to the Lord in relation to His things, and the Lord becomes even our bodily life in relation to heavenly things. That is a fact. Therein is the testimony, that we are brought progressively, on the one hand, to the place where, in the Lord's things, we have no life in ourselves, where even physically we are faced with impossibility. It always has been so from God's standpoint, but we have been thinking that we were doing quite a lot because we had not been brought to the point where the consciousness of natural inability was allowed to overtake us. Now we have come to the place where, in greater or lesser degree, we realise that in the things of God we "cannot," even physically.

But if, on the one hand, eternal life operates to cut us off from our natural life as the basis of our relationship with God, on the other hand, it is perfectly wonderful what is done. It is "the Lord's doing, and it is marvellous in our eyes." The Lord even comes in as our physical life to the doing of more than would have been possible to us at our best, and certainly far beyond the present possibility, because He has made us know that as men we are nothing, even at our best. Life does that. Life forces off one system and brings on another, making room for it as it goes.

That, I believe is what the Lord meant when He said, "...I am come that they might have life, and that they might have it *more abundantly*" (John x. 10 KJV). We have thought that just to mean that we are to have abundance of exuberance. We are always asking for life more abundant that we might feel wonderfully elated and overflowing and energetic. The Lord is pre-eminently practical, and more abundant life means that, having life, you will find the need of more to lead you a little further, and you will need it abundantly as you go on, because that life alone can bring you into the fulness. And it is His will that there should be the full provision of life unto the full end, because the purpose is such an abundant purpose. The life is commensurate with the purpose.

All that and much more is bound up with this basic statement that the active principle of redemption is eternal life, and that while that redemption is perfect in Christ it is progressive in us by the principle of life, and that to come into the fulness of redemption for spirit, mind and body there has to be a constant increase of redemption life. This life is redeeming us all the time. It is redeeming us from this present evil age, from all that came in with Adam. Full redemption will be displayed when Christ appears, and we with Him, when seeing Him we shall be like Him. It will simply be the manifestation of that life which is His eternal life in us. Oh, the possibilities of that life to transfigure! As we look at the Lord Jesus on the Mount of Transfiguration we see the full display of the life which the Father gave to dwell in us. It blazes forth in its fulness there, and shows you what kind of a man that man is in whom Divine life is fully triumphant. He is a man full of glory, full of perfection; and when we see Him we shall be like Him.

The word for us as we close is this, that He has called us unto eternal life. We must lay hold on eternal life daily for spirit, and mind, and body.

TEN

THE HEAVENLY MAN
AND THE WORD OF GOD

Reading: Matthew iv. 4; John vi. 63, 68; viii. 47; xiv. 10; I Peter i. 23, 25; Hebrews iv. 12-13; I John iv. 17.

You will notice that what is said in the first four of these passages arises out of the fact that the Lord Jesus was the Heavenly Man. In the temptation in the wilderness, as recorded in the passage in Matthew, we see that it was following the opening of the heavens and the attestation from the Father, "This is my beloved Son..." that the enemy made his challenge to all that this designation of Christ as the Heavenly Man implied. "If thou art the Son...." The temptations had their foundation in the fact of the heavenliness of the Lord Jesus. In the passages in John's Gospel the same feature is seen. As we have already noted, John keeps in view the heavenliness of the Lord Jesus all the way through, from the first words of his Gospel to the end. The challenge of the Lord Jesus carries that same meaning: "Believest thou not that I am in the Father...." The Heavenly Man is brought before us at this point in relation to the Word of God.

We closed our previous meditation by dealing with the vital principle of redemption, and we were saying that that principle, which is eternal life, makes the redemption that is perfect in Christ, progressive in us. Redemption is introduced into us with the receiving of eternal life, and as the life operates, works, and increases, we come increasingly into the good of redemption. The real values of redemption become ours in experience by the operation of the life of the Redeemer in us, the Redeemer operating in us by His own life.

CHRIST THE BEGINNING OF THE CREATION OF GOD

In John xx. 22 we have an incident recorded which has given rise to a certain measure of perplexity: "...he breathed on them, and saith unto them, Receive ye the Holy Spirit." We perhaps want an explanation of that act, and of those words, and I think the explanation is that what He did and said was in pattern, and not immediately in actuality; that is, it was a representative act on the part of the last Adam. John xx sees us on resurrection ground with the Lord Jesus. We remember that it is written, "The first man Adam became a living soul. The last Adam became a life-giving spirit" (I Corinthians xv. 45). That must, in spiritual reality, relate to His resurrection. Not in the full sense was He a life-giving spirit before the Cross, neither was He the last Adam before the Cross. All that was represented by, and summed up, in Him, but in the sense of generation, this only begins on resurrection ground. There in the fullest sense He becomes the last Adam, a life-giving spirit. So on resurrection ground He performs this representative or pattern act, and utters these representative words as the last Adam, fulfilling in the spiritual sense the words of Revelation iii. 14, "...the beginning of the creation of God." In the literal sense He was that at the beginning of this world. He was the beginning of the creation of God. That does not mean that He was the first one created by God; it means that He began the creation of God literally then, as to this world.

In the new creation He is taking that place in the spiritual sense: "...the beginning of the creation of God." In the beginning of the literal creation there was a breathing into man of the breath of lives. Now, as the last Adam, as a life-giving spirit, He breathes upon them. It is a typical act. It is the last Adam acting in a pattern-way in relation to the first members of the new creation, the beginning of the creation of God. He is typically infusing eternal life into the new creation. It is only a typical act, because the Spirit was not yet given. The full expression of it came later at Pentecost.

THE HEAVENLY MAN IN RELATION TO THE WORD OF GOD

Here is life in relation to the Heavenly Man in the full sense. We now come to bring all this life principle in the Heavenly Man into relation to the Word of God. The Word of God is very closely related to this life, and this life is very closely related to the Word of God, both of them as in the Heavenly Man, the life and the Word. So much is this so that they are not things in Him, but He is them. He is the Word, and He is the life; the life and the Word are in Him as His very being. Yet the Word is utterance as well as person. If you have taken the trouble to study the technique of the point that is raised in the use of the words "Logos" and "rema," you know how difficult it is always to differentiate between the two. You know how they run into one another, and how very often they meet and are one. So it is that the person has the word and the word is the word of the person. There is a difference, and yet they are both bound up with the person. We shall see as we go on what it means.

(A) BEGOTTEN BY THE WORD

In the first place, as we have been saying, the Lord Jesus as the Heavenly Man was begotten through the Word. The angel visited Mary and presented her with the Word of God, and waited for her to respond to it before there was any living result, and when, after consideration and fighting her battle through the problem and the difficulty, and the cost of it, she responded, "Behold, the handmaid of the Lord; be it unto me according to thy word," then the living Christ was implanted.

(B) TESTED BY THE WORD

In the temptation in the wilderness, it is clearly indicated to us that, in the background of things, it was the Word of God that was governing the Lord. Every temptation was met with the Word of God: "It is written...." Life was contingent upon the Word of God: "Man shall not live by bread alone, but by every word that proceedeth out of the mouth of God" (Matthew iv. 4). In the Heavenly Man the life question is bound up with the Word of God. If you take the opposite of that, you know that the earthly man dies because he refuses the Word of God; his life depends upon the Word of God and his attitude toward it. Here the last Adam is taken up on the same basis, and inasmuch as He met the three temptations with the Word of God, it is perfectly clear that His life was bound up with the Word of God. It was the Word of God that was governing this whole experience, and its issue. The Heavenly Man was being assailed with a view to tearing Him out of His heavenly life, as it were, by getting Him in some way to refuse, or violate, or ignore the Word of God. He maintained His position as the Heavenly Man in life on the ground of the Word of God.

(C) GOVERNED BY THE WORD

Not only was He begotten through the Word, and tested by the Word, but in the third place, Christ was governed throughout the whole of His life by the Word of God. All the Law and the Prophets apply to Him. Said He to Jewish leaders, "Ye search the scriptures, because ye think that in them ye have eternal life; and these are they which bear witness of me" (John v. 39). The suggestion there does not immediately affect our consideration, but is worth noting. In effect He was saying: In your searching of the Scriptures for eternal life, it is the Person in the Scriptures that you need to know; it is in Him in whom the Scriptures are gathered up that eternal life is found. That is the force of the statement: "...these are they which bear witness of me." Again, when with the two on the way to Emmaus after His resurrection, it is said of Him that "beginning from Moses and from all the prophets, he interpreted to them in all the scriptures the things concerning himself."

We mark the fact, then, that all the Scriptures applied to Him. He embodied and fulfilled all the Scriptures. How often will He say, while here on the earth, concerning a certain movement, a certain act, a certain experience, a certain statement, "...that the scripture might be fulfilled...." If you have never taken out every instance in which that occurs, you should do so. It is worth gathering up.

THE RELATION OF THE HOLY SPIRIT TO THE WORD OF GOD AND THE HEAVENLY MAN

Now I want you to note this. The Lord Jesus, in the whole of His life, was being governed by the Word of God. How necessary it was, then, for Him to walk in the Spirit, so that the Word of God should be fulfilled. Now what does that mean? Take, for example, the Old Testament. Do you suppose for one moment that every statement in the Old Testament was always present in the mental consciousness of the Lord Jesus, and that when He went to do something He referred to His manual, and said: "Now shall I do this, or shall I do that? What does the Scripture say I ought to do?" Yet every part of the Scripture was controlling His life, and there was a sense in which He was responsible for everything there. It all applied to Him. But He was not carrying all the Scriptures in His head, nor even in a book, and referring to His memory or His manual for His conduct, His utterances, His acts, His experiences, for what He allowed and what He did not allow, for what He did and what He did not. Although the Word of God was with Him richly, although He would have had a great knowledge of the Scriptures—and that becomes perfectly clear as we read His utterances—that is not the way in which the Word of God governed Him; as though He had to call Scriptures to remembrance on every occasion and to act accordingly. He was moving in the Spirit of life, and as He did so He moved according to the Word of God. When necessary the Spirit of life brought the Word of God to His remembrance, and He was able to use it. How He did use it! But apart from any quoting of Scripture, and apart from any present memory of the particular passage which governed any given incident, the Spirit was moving with life, in relation to the Word of God. He was governed by the Word of God, so that even when, as Man, He was helpless upon the Cross, unable to do anything, it says of those very conditions, "…that the scripture might be fulfilled…." Again, it is recorded that when He was dead on the Cross, and they came to break the legs of those crucified, finding Him already dead, they break not His legs, "…that the scripture might be fulfilled, A bone of him shall not be broken" (John xix. 36). That Man is under the government of the Word of God in everything because of the Spirit possessing, because of the Spirit directing, and the Spirit taking responsibility.

I can see a danger there, and am going to safeguard what we are saying, but let us first of all stress this law. If we are walking in the Spirit, and are moving according to the life of the Heavenly Man, our lives will be ordered according to the Word of God. Sometimes we shall not know the Scripture that applies to a given moment, but we shall know of something happening; we shall know that at that point we were checked; it was as though within us something said: "That is not right, you will have to correct that statement; there is a flaw in that, and you will have to make that good." How often we have known that. Afterwards we have discovered where we were mistaken. The Spirit of life does not let anything that is contrary to the Word of God pass, if we are walking in the Spirit. Surely that should be a great comfort to us, and a great help.

THE WORD OF GOD NEVER TO BE SET ASIDE

But there is a danger of which we need to beware. What we have said does not mean that we can take up a course of trying to walk in the Spirit, and neglect the Word of God. We cannot say: "Well, to walk in the Spirit is all we need and we shall be according to the Word of God; we need not bother about that." There are a lot of people who live in what they call their "spirit." They "get it from the Lord." They get something, and act upon it, and afterwards it is discovered that it is a direct violation of the Word of God. How often we have met that. People get things "from the Lord," and do something which they think they got from the Lord, and it is as clear as possible that the Word of God is positively against what they have done.

Thus the matter needs safeguarding. "Let the word of Christ dwell in you richly; in all wisdom..." (Colossians iii. 16) as a basis for the Holy Spirit. If, however, you are doing that you will not always have the exact passage to hand to govern the thing of the moment, but the Holy Spirit will be making good in you what He knows to be the Word of God, and holding you up. How true that is. Some of us have found that our natural memories have in great measure broken down. Very often a misquotation of Scripture does not touch doctrine at all, but the point is this, that there is a governing Intelligence which makes us know the Word of God, though we may not be able for the moment to give a particular passage in its exact phrasing or call it to mind. We are governed by it if we belong to the Heavenly Man. "...As he is, even so are we in this world" (I John

iv. 17). Here is the Heavenly Man governed by the Word of God, inasmuch as there was life in Him.

What is true of the Head, is to be true of the members. If we are to be joined to the Heavenly Man, we become parts of that corporate Heavenly Man, and that same life is in us, and we shall walk by the Word. We shall be governed by the Word through the Spirit of life that is in the Word, and that Spirit of life is all-knowing, all-intelligent. I wish that all the Lord's people lived on that basis. It would save us from all that deadly heresy-hunting kind of thing, from always being suspicious, little, doctrinal watch-dogs, keeping a look-out for anything that is erroneous, and producing a blight of death over everything. If we were but living in the Spirit, we should know in our hearts whether a thing were right or not, without projecting our analytical minds into things; the Spirit would bear witness in our hearts. That would be life and salvation. The other is a miserable existence for everybody.

Now you see the Heavenly Man, eternal life, and the Word governing throughout. What a difference there is between being governed by the letter and being governed by the Spirit. We may have the book; may possess all the letter; and may be constantly exclaiming, "To the law and to the testimony!" We may thus become very legal, checking up on the letter all the time. The Lord Jesus did not thus act, nor did the Apostle Paul. Zealous as they were for the Scriptures, for the Word of God, utterly governed by the Word of God, the thing which mattered with them was the living Word. Said our Lord Jesus: "...the words that I have spoken unto you are spirit, and are life"; "...the flesh profiteth nothing" (John vi. 63). We can kill with the letter. We can kill with the Word, as the Word. Surely we want to be delivered from dealing with the Scriptures as words, as letters, and to be brought into the place where it is the Spirit in the Word giving life. What a difference there is between those two realms. One leads to nothing but death, paralysis, to the chilling and blighting of everything; the other leads to a positive condemnation, to judgment which is necessary to slay the thing that is evil. It does not leave things in that blighted state without any meaning, which is all too often the case when it is merely a thing of the letter.

So you get the twofold aspect of the Word unto growth in Christ. Firstly, the Word is a Spirit-breathed utterance. That is what the Word of God must be, and not just something that has been written. Secondly, the Spirit of life associated with the Word. This raises a very big question, a question that perhaps it is almost dangerous to open in public in these days, and to answer which maybe would require a good deal of explanation. The question is this: How far is the written Word, as it stands, the Word of God? This Book can be taken hold of and the same fragment used in fifty different ways at the same time. The same passage of Scripture can be the basis of a dozen different things, all of which are mutually exclusive and contradictory. Which of these dozen or fifty is the Word of God? You can take Scripture as the letter like that, out from this Book, and you can say: This is the Word of God! How are you going to prove it? All these different people take the Word of God, and get a different meaning with a different result, act in a different way, and justify a different course, and the same Word has brought about terrific conflict and opposition between different sections of people. How far is it the Word of God as it stands? My point is this, that I believe that something extra is necessary to make that the Word of God in truth, in fulness, and that is the Spirit of life in it. That Spirit of life (we are thinking of the Holy Spirit now, not an unintelligent abstraction) must Himself use, and apply, that Word, to make it the Word of God. I do not believe that you can get any Divine result by simply quoting scripture as scripture. The Holy Spirit has to come into that Word, express Himself as in it, and make it live before you get the Divine result, because of the object in view. A living Heavenly Man is not made by mere words, even though they be words of Scripture. That is what people have tried to do. They have tried to make the Church by words of Scripture, constitute the Church by what is here as written, and so you have half a dozen different kinds of churches, all standing on what they call the Word of God, and the thing does not live. It is a living, Heavenly Man that God has in view, and to produce that, the Spirit must operate through the Word. "The words that I have spoken unto you are spirit, and are life," said the Lord to His disciples. "Lord, to whom shall we go? thou hast the words of eternal life." On the part of Peter, the spokesman of these latter words, this was a word of discrimination. The scribes and Pharisees had the Scriptures. They claimed that everything they had and held was in the Word of God. Ah yes, but they knew them not as the words of eternal life. There is a difference. This life is in His Son. It has to be in a living relationship to the Lord Jesus that the Scriptures are made effective.

THE SOVEREIGNTY OF GOD IN THE CREATIVE WORD

That works, in the first place, sovereignly in the direction of the unsaved. You may take the Word of God as it is written and preach it, but you have to leave the whole matter to the sovereignty of the Spirit. Preach it to a crowd of fifty, a hundred, a thousand, and to nine hundred and ninety-nine of the thousand the thing is as dead as anything can be. They see nothing, they feel nothing, but one in the thousand is sovereignly touched. That word is something more than an utterance, than letters, that word is spirit and life. That is no accident, no chance, but a sovereign act. The Spirit of God has come into the Word in relation to that one. That is the foolishness of preaching, in a sense, that you have to preach, and have no guarantee that the many will be touched by the Word of God. You have to commit yourself to the waters, and believe that God will somewhere come into the Word and touch some life, though the majority should be left untouched. That is the extra element, the Spirit of life in the Word of God, sovereignly acting in relation to the unsaved.

That, of course, is the creative Word, and brings us to see that in the Heavenly Man the Word of God is God's act, and not just God's statement. In the Heavenly Man the Word of God is never a statement alone, it is an act. We say many things, and then we look round for the result, with the thought in our minds, "What is the value of all this?" You have never, never to look for the result of God's Word in the Heavenly Man; it is there. You may not see it, but it is there. The Word in relation to the Spirit of life in Christ is an act; something is done; and when that Word has come by the Spirit of life, those to whom it has been directed by the intelligent Spirit can never again be the same, though they may seem to go on in the old way: "…the word that I spake, the same shall judge him in the last day" (John xii. 48). Something has been said; the Word has come, and the thing is done, never to be undone. Sooner or later those concerned are going to come right up against that, and it is all going to be dated back to the hour when the Spirit gave expression to the Word. That is a tremendous fact. That is the value of giving the Word in the Spirit, because it is an act. It is creative. It is something done, not something said. Oh, to recognise that the Word in the Holy Ghost is something done, not merely something said. God's Word is always God's act: "…the worlds have been framed by the word of God…" (Hebrews xi. 3). The Word of the Lord *is* a blessing. It is not just saying, "The Lord bless you." It is a blessing in itself; it brings the blessing. It is an act.

THE LIFE PRINCIPLE ESTABLISHED IN THE CASE OF THE SAVED

In the saved there is another side. The first side is creative, sovereign. Now in the case of the saved, where those concerned are the Lord's people, the operation of the Spirit in relation to the Word of God is no longer purely sovereign. In the case of believers the Word is not given with a view to bringing about creation, for that is done. We stand because of the Word of the Lord spoken sovereignly by the Spirit into our hearts, having thus been made His children, begotten by the Word of God. That is a sovereign act, but from that time onward, that which is sovereign ceases and growth is by the Spirit of life in the Word; but upon a basis that there is life in us to correspond to the life in the Word. The life in the one, or in the company, concerned is the basis of growth according to the Word of the Lord, which has life in itself. Take a simple illustration from our use of natural food. No matter how you may feed a corpse, you will get no development, no kind of growth. It is of no use feeding a dead man. There must be some life in a man that corresponds to the life in the food, takes hold of it, works with it, co-operates with it, before there can be growth. That is what we mean by the activity which bears the mark of sovereignty in the main ceasing. The sovereign act is something apart from ourselves; it is the grace of God to sinners who can give nothing back. Now that the life is in us our growth is on the basis of the life within us co-operating with the life in His Word. You can preach to people who have not much light, and preach in the Holy Ghost, and may not get very much result because of the limited measure of life that is in them. But you get tremendous response to a living word when people are all alive unto the Lord, when there is life in them. Growth comes that way, the life in us corresponding to the life in the Word, forming the Heavenly Man.

The Spirit-accompanied Word imparts life, quickens into life where there is a dead state, and does it sovereignly; but the Spirit-accompanied Word requires a response in the spirit in the case of those who have already been sovereignly brought into relation to Christ through the Word. The same life in the Word governs our lives as governed our new birth. The Lord Jesus was begotten truly of the Holy Ghost, the Spirit of life, but by the Word, or through the Word. Now, for the governing of His life, the same life through the Word operated as in the birth; that is, the same life that brought into being must be in the Word which governs the life, to bring that being to full growth. It is the life principle which is so important. It is this newness, this freshness that is of such account—if you like, this originality. Do not misunderstand; we are not using that word in the natural sense. We mean that in the birth by the Spirit of life there is something that never was before; it is original, new. We are a new creation in Christ Jesus. We call it the "new birth." It is not just something fresh, recent, but something that was not before.

In relation to the Word it has to be like that. The Word must come with all the force of something that never was before. There has to be a sense of Divine originality and freshness about it that is bringing to wonder, amazement. Again, you can test that. When the Word is in the hands of the Holy Spirit, though you may have read a passage a thousand times, and have had something from that word, you can come back to it again and say: "Well, I never saw that before! Why, this is alive with meaning and value beyond anything before!" There is all the difference between that, and the stale stuff that we put into books as the result of our Bible study. The Lord

would have His ministers in the realm where their handling of the
Word of God is in life. It is the Heavenly Man being governed by the
heavenly life in the Word, so that everything is constantly new, constantly fresh, constantly original.

How true that is to experience. There have been times when we
thought we knew all about a certain thing in the Bible; we have
talked about it tremendously, and it has been our theme for a long
time. Then a period of time has elapsed when we have left it, and the
Spirit of the Lord has led us to that again, and it is as though we have
never seen that truth before. We find that we can come back to the
old themes, as they are called, with such a newness. Other people
may not realise what is going on in us. They may hear what amounts
to the old things again, but they say: "There is such a new meaning,
a new grip, that it is quite clear the Holy Spirit has not finished with
that matter, and has more to say to us about it." We have to be careful how we react mentally to things like that. We are so often tempted to take this attitude: "Oh, well, I have spoken of that so often that
people must be tired of it!" The Holy Spirit is saying: "You say it
again; do not take any notice of what they think; if they have heard
it a thousand times, you say it!" And when you do so, there is something done which, with all the earlier utterances of the same thing,
has never been done before. Be careful of pigeon-holing anything in
the Word of God, and saying that we have exhausted that. If you are
dealing with the themes of the Bible, as such, you may as well
pigeon-hole the whole thing right away. If you are moving in the
Spirit with the Word of God, there will never be a time when any part
of the Word of God becomes obsolete. It is the same new life that
never was before, which came into us to constitute us a part of the
Heavenly Man, which is so governed by the Word all the way along,
unto constant increase, constant growth.

Remember, then, that it is a matter of life. Remember that doctrine comes out of life, and not life out of doctrine. The Church comes
out of life, and not life out of the Church. It is not attachment to doctrine, nor attachment to the Church, but attachment to the Heavenly
Man in a living way that is the vital necessity; and then you will get
the doctrine and the Church. In the Word as we have it, the doctrine
came after the life. The Church existed before the doctrine of the

Church was given. Attachment to the Heavenly Man produced the doctrine of the Church. The Church came about by a living relationship, not by taking up a revelation of what the Church was, and seeking to put it into operation. Life comes first of all, and where life is found the rest will follow. It is of no use trying to impose the doctrine of the Church, or any other doctrine, upon people, if they are not alive unto the Lord. The Lord knows what He is doing. You cannot go about the world anywhere, not even amongst Christian people, with your full doctrine, your full revelation, and have the assurance that, as you give it out, they are going to leap to it. You have to go where the Spirit leads you, for the Spirit knows exactly where there is a sufficiency of life to have prepared the ground, and what can respond to that which you have to give. How we would like to go out into the world and talk to all the Lord's people of what He has shown us, and give them the revelation of the Body of Christ! We should go and organise great gatherings and get people together, only to find that they look at us blankly and exclaim: "This is strange doctrine!" You cannot do it like that. Increase has to be on a basis of life; because doctrine does not come first, but life. You cannot get the Church by trying to get it! There has to be life, and life by its working forms the Church, becomes the realisation of the Church. The reversal of that order only leads to Babylon.

What is Babylon? Babylon represents the loss of the authority of the Word of God as a living thing. It was in the reign of Jehoiakim, the king who took his penknife and cut up the Word of God, that Judah began to be carried away into Babylon. When he repudiated the living authority of the Word of God, all the vessels of gold and silver were carried off to Babylon. It is a parable. It means that the Lord's people come into bondage, into captivity, into death, are out of the place of the Lord's appointment, and the Lord's ministry is not going on in life, because the vessels have departed, have all been taken away. Right up to that time they were going on with their sacrifices, going on with their Levitical order. But that is not the point. You can have the form of things, the system, and yet go to Babylon. It is the Word of the Lord as a spiritual and living thing, which keeps you free, clear, strong, out of Babylon.

ELEVEN

THE HEAVENLY MAN
AND THE WORD OF GOD

(CONTD.)

Reading: John i. 14; xiv. 10; Colossians iii. 16, 17; Revelation xix. 13.

In the course of our previous meditation, we noted the relationship of the Holy Spirit to the Word of God and the Heavenly Man, and before we pass on to further considerations it may be well to sum up that relationship under three or four specific heads.

THE HOLY SPIRIT RELATED TO THE WORD OF GOD AND THE HEAVENLY MAN

(a) In Birth. We observe, then, that the Holy Spirit is related to the Word of God in the birth of the Heavenly Man. The Word was presented to Mary, and it created for her a problem. In the human realm there was perplexity as to how the realisation of this thing could be; how she should attain unto that; how this wonderful presentation and unveiling of possibility and meaning, purpose and intent, and Divine thought could ever become a realised thing. That was her problem. The angel answered her enquiry and cleared her perplexity with one statement: "…The Holy Spirit shall come upon thee…" (Luke i. 35). So we see that, related to the Word of God, there was the Spirit, in this birth.

The Holy Ghost did not take up the Word to make it a realised thing in Mary until she had committed herself to the Word. That is always a law. But when she committed herself deliberately to the Word, then the Holy Ghost took up the realisation of the meaning, the implication, the content, the purpose of that Word.

(b) In Conflict. In the same way the Holy Spirit was associated with the Word of God in the conflict. When the Spirit had come upon the Lord Jesus, as the Heavenly Man, at Jordan, He was led of the Spirit into the wilderness, to be tempted of the Devil. Being led of the Spirit, governed by the Spirit, actuated by, and moving in, the Spirit, the Word of God was, by the Spirit, the instrument for the overthrow of the enemy, and for the ultimate advance rather than the arrest of the Heavenly Man. You notice that there is the mark of enlargement, because when the Devil left Him, it says, "...Jesus returned in the power of the Spirit..." (Luke iv. 14). There is the mark of enlargement, the sign of increase through this that has happened. The Spirit was associated with the Word in the conflict, unto victory, and unto enlargement.

(c) In Ministry. The same was true in the ministry of the Lord Jesus: "...the words that I say unto you I speak not from myself: but the Father abiding in me doeth his works" (John xiv. 10). The words are the issue of an indwelling activity of the Father, by the Spirit.

We are speaking solely of Christ as the Heavenly Man now, not of Christ in His Deity and Godhead, as the Son of God in the highest sense. In His ministry, by the anointing, by the indwelling Spirit of the Father, there are activities going on in Him which result in words coming from Him. But they are not from Him apart from the Father, they are not from Him out of relationship with the Spirit, they are coming from the inward activities and energies of the Spirit of the Father. The Spirit is producing the words by His operations in the life. That is why they are always practical words, that is, words of practical effect. We will come back to that presently.

(d) In the Life. What was true in His spoken ministry, and in these other ways, was also true in His life. His life was a continuous and spontaneous fulfilling of the Scriptures, not by continuous reference to them, but through the indwelling of the Spirit, who had the Scriptures in possession, having Himself given them, and inspired them. They are eternal, and the Spirit in Him was moving in such a

way that the Scriptures were being fulfilled all the time. On many occasions the statement is made to indicate that fact: "...that the scripture might be fulfilled...." So He was energised and actuated in His life, and in all its incidents, by the Spirit in relation to the Word. The Heavenly Man is governed by the Word of God through the Eternal Spirit. That is true of Him personally.

Now that is true also of Him corporately. The corporate Heavenly Man is the result of the same process. The Church, His Body, in its every part, is brought into being by the Word, firstly presented, and then contemplated, considered, responded to, and the Holy Ghost taking it up and making it a living thing. The result is the Church, the Body of Christ, the corporate Heavenly Man.

That is how the Church comes into being, and to contemplate any kind of thing called the Church, which does not come in by the operation of the Holy Spirit through the Word of God, is to contemplate something that does not exist in the thought of God. Set the Word of God aside and you will have no Church. What you will have is something that is utterly false. Set the Holy Ghost, in relation to the Word of God, aside, and you destroy what you are trying to build up.

That is viewing it in a very general way, but for us it becomes an immediate matter that our very being, as a part of Christ, issues from exactly the same principle as operated in His incarnation, the Word and the Spirit co-operating.

A REITERATION OF THE DIVINE PURPOSE—THE PRINCIPLE OF INCARNATION

Let us break this up, going back a little in thought. God requires a Man for the expression of His thoughts. To put that in another way, God has never meant just to utter words, statements; to make Himself known and give expression to Himself by verbal utterances. There is a great deal more hanging upon that than appears for the moment, but that is the simple fact, that God has never intended to make Himself known by statements, by words, by verbal utterances. That is why it is infinitely perilous to be occupied with teaching as teaching, and to take up teaching as teaching, to take up things said, and think that because we have the thing said to us we have the thing itself. We never have! Many people have all the things that have been said, but they have not the thing itself. There is such a position to come to as that of learning, and never coming to a knowledge of the truth. That is a position of great peril. Yes, for twenty, thirty, forty, fifty years we may have heard all that there is, and know it all, and yet never have come to a knowledge of the truth. It sounds like a contradiction, but it is possible, or the Word of God would not say so. What is the trouble? Where is the flaw? That is what we are trying to see now.

Now, as we have said, God never intended to try to make Himself known, to give expression to Himself, by words, by statements, by mere utterances, that is, by things said. For the expression of His thoughts God requires a Man. The Word, therefore, becomes flesh; for the man God desires must be the product of His Word in an inward way; that is, life must be related to truth, and truth must be related to life.

Again, there is the terrible danger of speaking apart from the Word of God having been inwrought. There is a fascination about the great truths, and connected with this there is a danger, especially if you happen to be in what is called "ministry." The danger is that of getting hold of truths, of doctrines, of themes, of subjects, of things in the Word of God, and all the time talking about them. You go and hear something fresh, and it is a new idea, and so off you go to give it out. In reality you are collecting material for your ministry in that way, and there is a terrible danger in so doing. It is going to put you and your hearers into a false position. As we have already said, it will make things top-heavy. You are building teaching upon something that is not life, that is not growth. It is simply a case of putting teaching on to people, and presently the whole thing will topple over, down will come your edifice, and you will wonder what is the matter. It is only life that counts. You have to lay a foundation, but there must be an excavating, an upheaving, a breaking up, an inworking, before you can add teaching. That is why doctrine followed the working of grace in the heart, in the New Testament. The word of grace was begun, and then the Lord explained by the doctrine what He had been doing. It is often thus with ourselves. The Lord takes us through something which we cannot understand, and which to us, while we are passing through it, is a deep, dark, terrible experience, but afterward He explains it to us in His Word, and we are brought into a full interpretation of what we have gone through. It is far better to have it so.

The receiving of the Word of God by the Old Testament prophets is described by the Hebrew verb *hayah*, which means "happened." Thus the literal rendering of the Hebrew is, "The word of the Lord *happened* unto so and so." In our translation this is expressed by the word "came": "The word of the Lord *came* to so and so." It is an event, not just a verbal utterance. That is how it has to be through us to others. That is why the Lord said, "…the words that I have spoken unto you are spirit, and are life…" (John vi. 63). There is an event with His words, not always in the immediate consciousness of those spoken to, but, as we have already pointed out, something is done, and it will come to light one day. Upon that everything in destiny hangs. God speaks, and something is effected one way or the other. Thus the Word of God is not merely a saying, a speech, it is an event.

The full value is given to the Word of God when it is incorporated in a body. That is, of course, patent in the case of the Lord Jesus Himself. The full value of the Scriptures was reached when they were incorporated in Him personally, when it could be said, "And the Word became flesh, and dwelt among us…full of grace and truth" (John i. 14).

THE WORD OF GOD AND A LIVING ASSEMBLY

On the corporate side there is something to be recognised which perhaps may occasion difficulty for the moment, but which is nevertheless true, and something that must be taken into account, and be remembered, that the Word of the Lord in a living assembly has special value and power. If you have not seen that mentally, and recognised that as a truth, possibly you have known it as an experience, as a fact. In a living assembly of the Lord's people, with the Word of the Lord in the midst, what power that Word has, and what value. But how unprofitable it is to try to preach the Word in the midst of an assembly that is not living, but dead and dry. It may be the Word of the Lord, and, so far as the preacher is concerned, it may be in the power of the Holy Ghost, but of how little profit it is. When you get an assembly really alive unto the Lord, a body throbbing with life, what value, what power, what fruit there is in the Word. It was true in the case of the Lord Jesus. There you have a living One, with the Word of God in Him, and you see how, so far as He was concerned, the Word was spirit and life. The Word had special value in Him, because in Him was life.

That is a true principle in relation to the Heavenly Man, as corporately set forth. You have there a living body, with the Lord's life and the Lord's Word in the midst, running, having free course, and being glorified. On the outer fringe of that company there may be the unsaved, and others who are not alive to the Spirit, but the fact that the Lord has a nucleus of living ones in the midst gives to the Word something of value, which makes it far more powerful, far more effective, than where this is not the case. This is a thing that those who minister in the Spirit know all about in experience. If the Word is ministered in a fairly large company, not very far advanced, and not having learned the language of the Spirit, and anything is said very much beyond early simplicities, they look at you almost open-mouthed, and think you are talking a strange language. But when the Word has been released and there have been two or three who are alive to the Word, it has taken on power, and these people, although not perhaps understanding the terminology, have become alive to something. Some of you when preaching may have looked round the congregation to find one co-operating spirit, and the Word has found release. If there is a nucleus in the midst of a realm of death, or comparative death, the Word of God has a special value by reason of a Holy-Spirit-actuated unit. It is there that we have to see the importance of being alive unto the Lord for the ministry.

We have been dealing with the fourth chapter of Ephesians, where we read of the Heavenly Man giving gifts; apostles, prophets, evangelists, pastors and teachers, for the perfecting of the saint unto the work of the ministry. The saints are to minister. Now here is a way in which the saints minister. All the saints do not come up on to the platform and give the message, but they marvellously minister when they co-operate with the ministry, and really the ministry of the apostle or prophet, evangelist, pastor or teacher, is fulfilled by the living company. It is a poor look-out for the one who is ministering, if there is not a company to fulfill the ministry like that, by spiritual co-operation. In that way the Lord gets through with a revelation of Himself. How much more can the Lord reveal Himself when He has a living company.

The Lord seemed severely limited when He was here, so that He could never say all He wanted to say: "I have yet many things to say unto you, but ye cannot bear them now" (John xvi. 12). Nor again, could He do what He wanted to do: "And he did not many mighty works there because of their unbelief" (Matthew xiii. 58). But, given a living company, there is no end to the possibilities. The Lord can reveal and express Himself there. The Lord needs a Man, a Heavenly Man, for His self-revelation, the expression of His thoughts, and the full value is only given to the Word when it is incorporated in a body.

CHRIST AND THE WORD OF GOD ARE ONE

Now we come much closer. The thing that must be said at once is, that by the Holy Spirit the Word is Christ. It is not a statement of things, it is the expression of a Person. What we mean to say is, that we have to take the same attitude toward the Word, that we take toward Christ. We have to face the Word of the Lord in the same way that we face the Lord Himself. It is not something of the Lord presented to us in words, but it is the Lord Himself coming to us. We cannot reject any part of His Word and keep Him. We cannot divide between the Lord and His Word. People seem to think that they can take some of the things the Lord has said and leave others. The Word is one. The Word is the Lord. To refuse the Word in any part, is to refuse the Lord, is to limit the Lord, is to say, in effect: "Lord, I do not want You! Lord, I will not have You!" It is not that we will not have the Word, but that we will not have the Lord Himself, for the two are one: "...his name is called The Word of God" (Revelation xix. 13). And "The Word became flesh..." (John i. 14). You cannot get in between, the two are one. He is the Word of God. God does not come to us in statements, He comes to us in Person, and the challenge is to take an attitude, not towards the things said, but towards the Lord Himself.

THE NECESSITY FOR HEART EXERCISE

The question that arises in most of our hearts when we have been hearing a great deal is, How is that to become our life? How is that to become a part of us? How are we to become the living expression of that? That is the question which should arise, at any rate. Let us remind ourselves, and those for whom we have responsibility in ministry, that it is possible to be ever learning, and never coming to a knowledge of the truth. We can attend conferences, go right through every meeting, and mentally take in all that is said, and go away with it in our minds, or have it in our notebooks, and then have to come back to another conference to get more, and then to another, and still another. We look back over the years of conferences and begin to take stock, and we ask ourselves the question: "What is the result of all this?" I remember that on such and such an occasion, such and such a thing was spoken about, and on another occasion something else; these have been the things which have been the subject of the various conferences; and now, what does it represent? That is a very solemn question. Is it that we know these things; that is, if they were repeated, should we take the attitude: "Well, we have heard that before; we know that!" That is what we mean by ever learning, ever learning, without maybe ever coming to the knowledge of the truth, in the sense in which that word "knowledge" is used. What are we going to do? How is all this to be translated into something more than words, more than thoughts, more than ideas, more than truths as truths, more than teaching, so that it really does become incorporated, expressed in a Man? It can be, and it must be. Exactly the same principle must operate as when Christ was born of Mary. It means that the Word presented has to lead us to exercise of heart. That is what happened with Mary. She immediately entered into an exercise of heart about it. You know what measure of exercise has resulted from your hearing of the Word. Consider it thus:

What does that mean? What does that involve? What cost will that entail? What is that going to lead to? Is that the will of God for me? The need is of a present, direct, and deliberate taking up of the Word, and facing it, contemplating it, entering into exercise of heart about it. That is the first step towards incarnation of the Word.

Having looked at it, having been exercised by it, we must take a deliberate step in relation to it in faith. That is necessary. You will never get anywhere unless you do. When, having faced that Word, weighed it, looked at it in the light of God's will for you, and having come to a position you take a deliberate attitude, if it is to be towards the Lord, the attitude must be: "Behold, the handmaid of the Lord [behold, the servant of the Lord]; be it unto me according to thy word." "I do not know how it can be; it seems an impossible thing, too high for me, but be it unto me." That is faith. Mary did not stand back and say: "Well, it is a wonderful revelation, far too great for me; I do not believe it can ever be, I cannot really accept it!" Wonderful as it was, and impossible as it was on any other ground but God, with the sheer impossibility of its ever being on any natural ground, she said: "Nevertheless, be it!" That is faith. It is not according to what I think is possible, what I feel to be possible, what seems to me to be possible, but "according to thy word." It is according to the Word, and that Word is not an impossible thing! If You have spoken, You do not speak impossibilities, You do not challenge me with impossibilities! "...be it unto me according to thy word." It is a committal of faith, a deliberate act of faith in relation to the Word, that is required.

How many of us have so acted over things which we have heard? How many of us have got away and, in exercise of heart, said: "Lord, that is a tremendous thing, and for me in a natural way it is quite impossible; but it is Your Word, therefore, be it unto me. I stand on it, and I stand for it, You make it good. I can do no more than say, Yes, and I believe God." There is a great deal in a transaction like that. Without that we do not grow. Without that we are ever learning and never coming to a knowledge of the truth. Without that so much of the truth becomes merely mental in its apprehension, and is not living, is not effective.

However much we have failed in the past, there is something to be done in this matter. When the Lord has been speaking to us, we should make it our first business to get apart with Him. You would not believe the heart-break it is, to one who has been pouring out that Word, to find that almost before he has finished his message, and the gathering is closed, people are talking on all the trivialities of their domestic and business affairs, on things that can quite well wait. It is not as though there were any serious or critical situation to be enquired into, but mere talk ensues long the lines of ordinary, every-day things. Our point is that there has to be a deliberate transaction with the Lord, if that Word is to become an expression of God in a life; and God can never be satisfied with anything else. God can never be satisfied with mere statements, but only with the man as a living expression of His words.

THE RELATION OF THE WORD TO THE CROSS

That is why the Word is always related to the Cross. The Apostle Paul uses this phrase: "For the word of the cross is…the power of God" (I Corinthians i. 18). It is the power of God. It is the wisdom of God. We know that the word used is the "Logos" of the Cross. The Logos is the combination of a thought and expression in a personal way. It is the Word in a Person, related to the Cross. That is why it is put in this way by the same Holy Spirit of knowledge and understanding, in the Book of the Revelation: "And he is arrayed in a garment [dipped in] blood: and his name is called The Word of God" (Revelation xix. 13). You see the two things, the garment sprinkled with blood, and His name "The Word of God." Then you look into the letter to the Hebrews, and you will remember that in chapter ix. 19, you have these words: "…he took the blood of the calves and the goats, with water and scarlet wool and hyssop, and sprinkled both the book itself and all the people." There is the Word and the Blood. It is the Cross that gives the working power to the Word.

The Cross of the Lord Jesus is a tremendously effective thing. The Cross of the Lord Jesus, in its spiritual value, will break down everything that stands in God's way. It will clear the ground of the old creation. It will destroy the power of the enemy and his works.

The Cross is a tremendous thing for breaking down, destroying, overthrowing. The Cross, on its resurrection side, knows no bounds to power: "...the exceeding greatness of his power to us-ward who believe, according to that working of the strength of his might which he wrought in Christ, when he raised him from the dead..." (Ephesians i. 19, 20). The Cross has these two sides, the breaking down side and the raising up side, and it is in the power of the Cross of the Lord Jesus that the Word of God finds its effectiveness. He becomes the Word of the Cross, and the garment sprinkled with blood is the garment of Him who is "The Word of God," and as "The Word of God" He gets His power by way of the Cross. Christ crucified is the power of God. When the Cross has its place in our lives, the Word of God is tremendously potent. An uncrucified preacher is an ineffective and unfruitful preacher. Ministry in the Word of God from any but a crucified minister or vessel is impotent, fruitless, barren. Find the crucified man giving the Word of God, and you know it will be effective, fruitful, powerful.

Take Jeremiah as a great Old Testament illustration. If ever there was a crucified man in spirit, it was Jeremiah. He bears the marks of a crucified man right from the beginning. If you want to know what a crucified man is, read the first chapter of Jeremiah's prophecy, and you will see him indicated at once. Read right through Jeremiah, and you will see a life-size portrait of a crucified man. Turn to chapter i. 4-6:

Now the word of Jehovah came unto me, saying, Before I formed thee in the belly I knew thee, and before thou camest forth out of the womb I sanctified thee; I have appointed thee a prophet unto the nations.

Any natural, uncrucified man would leap at that, and say: "My! I am somebody! What power is entrusted to me! What a life-work I have!"

Then said I, Ah, Lord God! behold, I cannot speak: for I am a child (KJV).

Such is the reaction of a crucified man to a great prospect set before him by the Lord. See what a crucified man can be when the Lord has him in His hands—verses 9, 10:

"...I have put my words in thy mouth: see, I have this day set thee over the nations and over the kingdoms, to

pluck up and to break down and to destroy and to over-
throw, to build and to plant."

There is the Cross in the word of the crucified man: "...my words in
thy mouth..." destroying, overthrowing, plucking up, casting down.
That is the power of the Cross. The Lord does that with regard to ourselves. The Cross works havoc in our flesh. It brings us to an end.
But there is another side of the Cross, and that is to build, and to
plant. That is the working of the Cross in resurrection. Thus we have
the Word in the mouth of a crucified man. It is the Word of the Cross
in effect. It is Christ crucified, the power of His Cross bringing into
view a Heavenly Man, through the embodiment of the Word of God.
The Cross gets rid of that other man who looms so large, and who is
to be summed up in Antichrist, the super-man, who will sit in the
very temple of God giving out that he is God; some great one of this
old and cursed creation, so lifted up in pride that he assumes the very
place of God. The Cross casts him out, and brings God's man into
view, greater than he. Over against Antichrist is Christ, and there is
no comparison. The Cross brings in that Man by putting out the
other. All that is in us of that other man the Cross brings to nought,
and thus makes room for the revelation of the Heavenly Man, both
personally and corporately, and gives to us a ministry which is the
result of the work of His Word within. It is a ministry which is a
work, not a ministry of statements. That is why we have stressed the
words in John xiv—"...*the words* that I say unto you I speak not
from myself: but the Father abiding in me doeth his works." The
Father dwelling in Him was doing His works. The words that He
speaks, He is not speaking from Himself, they are coming out of the
Father's works. Thus, it is not a case of truth, teaching, words, ideas;
it is a ministry (evidenced, maybe, by words, but by "words...which
the Spirit teacheth") resultant from inward words, the works of the
Spirit within. The Lord lead us more into that.

Twelve

Taking the Ground
of the Heavenly Man

Reading: Colossians ii. 16-23; iii. 1-11; Ephesians iv. 13-15.

There is one particular application of this whole vast, comprehensive truth which we feel we should stress at this time. It has to do with our taking the ground of the Heavenly Man. Whether you consider Him personally or corporately in the Word, you will see that the one thing which is being pointed out as absolutely necessary, is that the ground of the Heavenly Man shall be taken; that is, that man shall come on to the ground of the Heavenly Man. God has nothing to say to men, nothing to do with them, on any other ground than that of the Heavenly Man. His attitude is that, if you want Him to speak to you, to have anything to do with you, you must come on to His ground, which is that of the Heavenly Man. You have to leave your own ground of nature, whatever be your thought of it, and you have to come on to His ground. You must leave the ground of the earthly man, the fallen Adam, leave natural ground, and come on to the ground of the last Adam, on to heavenly ground, which is spiritual ground.

If you were to take that thought, and begin to read again the Gospel by John, and then go on into the Epistles, especially those of Paul, although it is not confined to them, you would see that this is the one thing all the way through, and it would give you a wonderful opening up of the Word.

Christ the Sole Ground of God's Dealings With Man

We begin, then, by seeing that the Father has set forth the Son as His ground of dealing with men, and He will deal with no man on any other ground: "…him the Father, even God, hath sealed" (John vi. 27). Jesus of Nazareth was anointed by God. Now that is God's ground: "This is my beloved Son, in whom I am well pleased" (Matthew iii. 17); "This is my beloved Son…hear ye him" (Matthew xvii. 5). He has set forth the Son, and if you want to have anything to do with God at all, if you want Him to have anything at all to do with you, you have to come on to the ground of the Son, the ground of the Heavenly Man. God meets us in Him. God takes up His work with us there on that ground. God carries on His work with us on that ground alone. For all God's interest and activity with us, Christ is the first and the last. He is set forth, sealed, anointed, and there only shall we find an opened Heaven.

Referring again to Jacob and his dream, we read: "And he lighted upon a certain place, and tarried there all night.…And he dreamed. And behold, a ladder set up on the earth, and the top of it reached to heaven. And behold, the angels of God ascending and descending on it. And, behold, Jehovah stood above it, and said…" (Genesis xxviii. 11-13). The Lord took that up, as you remember, with Nathanael, and said: "…Ye shall see the heaven opened, and the angels of God ascending and descending upon the Son of man" (John i. 51). The Lord communes with man by way of that ladder, which is the Son of Man, and by way of His Son alone; He speaks to us at the end of these times "in his Son, whom he appointed heir of all things…" (Hebrews i. 2). I think it hardly needs stressing that this is where we begin, and this is what the Father has done. He has made the Heavenly Man, His Son, the sole ground upon which to meet man.

THE MEANING OF THE DIVINE APPOINTMENT OF THE SON

In using the term "Heavenly Man," we are doing something more than just referring to a Divine Person, the Son of God. We are implying a great order of Man, a kind of Man, constituted by all heavenly features, resources, faculties. Everything about this Man is heavenly, and of practical value. Nothing in Him is without meaning, without value. It is something of an applied kind; that is, everything that is in Christ is of use, of heavenly use for us, of heavenly value, of practical meaning. That is why we speak of Him as the Heavenly Man, the kind God has in view. God can only deal with that kind, and that is why we have to leave our own ground and get on to Christ's ground, because God can only deal with that kind. That is what is meant by the so familiar phrase, "Believe on the Lord Jesus..." (literally, believe on to the Lord Jesus). This is not the mere taking of an attitude toward Him and saying: "Of course I believe Him, I believe He is a perfectly trustworthy one." No! It is the committing of oneself, a stepping on to His ground, taking the ground of the Heavenly Man. Until that is done there is no hope at all. In order to do that, we have to leave our own ground, and that is not so simple as it sounds. It is a life-long education. There may be one act in the beginning, where in that first initial sense we believe on to the Lord Jesus Christ; where we step over on to Him in faith and commit ourselves to Him and trust Him, but for the rest of our lives we shall be learning what it is to leave our own ground and take His. As we do that we come to His fulness, the fulness of the stature of Christ. It is as we learn to leave our own ground and take the ground of the Heavenly Man that this can be. We have plenty of opportunities every day we live in which to do that. It is a life-long course, though there is that initial act in the beginning of which we have spoken.

THE TRUTH ILLUSTRATED IN THE CASE OF:
(A) NICODEMUS

Take some examples. Nicodemus presents himself to the Lord Jesus as interested in Divine things, interested in what he calls the kingdom of God. He feels that Jesus can tell him something, and give him some information. "Rabbi, we know that thou art a teacher come from God..." (John iii. 2). "Well, You can tell us something!" The Lord does not begin to give him information. He does not begin to satisfy his inquiries, and to open up to him Divine secrets. He makes no response to that inquiry, but He says, in effect: "Nicodemus, ruler of the Jews as you are, you have to leave that ground and to come on to another ground altogether; you must be born anew."

As you follow out the meaning of that conversation, and of what the Lord said, you see perfectly clearly that He is only saying in other words, "You have to come on to My ground. You must be where I am, before you can know what I know. You want to know what I know. Well, I cannot tell you, but you will know it if you are born again; you will have My heavenly knowledge when you occupy My heavenly ground. You can only occupy My heavenly ground by being born from above as I have been. It is a Heavenly Man's ground for a Heavenly Man's knowledge. You must leave your own ground." "What, leave my ground? What is wrong with my ground? I am a good, upright Israelite, a faithful teacher of the Law!" "Yes, but you have to leave that ground," the Lord Jesus would say; "I am not now dealing with a man and his standing with the Law, I am dealing with you, Nicodemus, a ruler in Israel; you have to leave your ground and come on to Mine."

That is what is clearly to be inferred from John iii and the same principle can be followed throughout the Gospel. That is the law which is being applied all the way through.

(B) THE INQUIRING GREEKS

You come to chapter xii and you read: "Now there were certain Greeks among those that went up to worship at the feast: these therefore came to Philip...and asked him, saying, Sir, we would see Jesus" (John xii. 20, 21). Then the disciples came and told the Lord Jesus that there were certain Greeks wanting to see Him. What did the Lord Jesus reply? Did He say: "Very well, I will come and show them Myself!" No! "And Jesus answereth them, saying, The hour is come, that the Son of man should be glorified. Verily, verily, I say unto you, Except a grain of wheat fall into the earth and die, it abideth by itself alone; but if it die, it beareth much fruit" (verses 23, 24). Did they want to see Him? They must come on to His ground. What is that ground? Heavenly ground, resurrection ground. It is not the ground of this creation, but you must needs die to get on to this ground. It is not the ground of this earthly life, but you must die to that. Those Greeks could never "see" Him if their thought of Him were as of someone of interest here on this earth; if they had come to see someone of whom they had heard wonderful things, and were looking for a wonderful man who has been performing miracles; if

He were as one of the sights of Jerusalem for which they had come to the feast, one of the people to get into touch with. They must leave that ground altogether, and leave it through death (we will come back to that again presently); then they shall see Him by corporate relationship: "...if it die, it beareth much fruit." One corn of wheat turned into an ear—and a harvest. That is how the Lord Jesus can be known, by our becoming a part of the corporate Heavenly Man, through death and resurrection. You have to leave the natural ground if you want to see Him. It is not by the contemplation of Him as a historical figure that you see Him; you only see Him by resurrection-union with Him, on the ground of the Heavenly Man.

How true that was with the disciples themselves. He was with them by the space of three and a half years, and yet they really did not know Him, and did not "see" Him; but after He had gone from them, they saw Him and knew Him. The knowledge was something far transcending that of the days of His flesh.

(C) PETER AND THE GENTILES

Come further, over into the early chapters of the Book of the Acts, and you come to that paragraph in the history of first things in the Church, where Peter has been fasting and praying. He falls into a trance and sees the heaven opened and a sheet let down from Heaven. In it are all manner of four-footed beasts and creeping things; and a voice says to him, "Rise, Peter; kill and eat" (Acts x. 13). To this Peter replied, "Not so, Lord; for I have never eaten anything that is common and unclean" (verse 14). We know what it is related to. Away up country there is a devout man with very little light, reaching out with all his heart to know the Lord more perfectly, to go on with God; hungry for the Lord, but not knowing the way. In his reaching out for the Lord, he is visited by an angel, and told that if he sends to a certain place, at such and such an address, there is a man there named Peter, who, if he but calls for him to come, will tell him what he needs to know. Meanwhile in connection with that man, who is not a Jew, who is not of Israel, and who is outside the covenant, the Lord is having these dealings with Peter. Now, to Peter, that man would be as one of those reptiles, those creeping things, as unclean meat, because he was outside Israel. Peter says, "Not so, Lord...." Now Peter must leave that ground. That is his old Jewish ground, and he must leave it and come on to the ground of the Heavenly Man. What is the ground of the Heavenly Man? It is that where there is neither Jew nor Greek, where these distinctions are not to be made. You are not to make these distinctions, Peter! You are not to stand off like this, saying, I am a Jew and he is not a Jew; we have no relationship! Fellowship is the mark of the Heavenly Man, and there these distinctions are lost sight of. You must come off your earthly, historic, traditional ground, Peter, on to the ground of the Heavenly Man.

The Lord made it perfectly clear that Peter had to do it, and that the issues were very serious and critical if he did not. Peter had the grace of obedience to leave his own ground, and he went up to Caesarea and met with one of the greatest surprises of his life in that he found that the Lord was there! He had to report to the other Jewish apostles that, though he had gone with all fear and misgiving, he found the Lord there. Yes, the Lord was on the ground that He Himself had provided, the ground of the Heavenly Man. We shall always meet the Lord on that ground. Leave your own ground, and come on to My ground, and I will meet you there and show you something which will surprise you. So it was in this case: "Who was I, that I could withstand God?" (Acts xi. 17). "The Lord had given them the Spirit, and I had to get off my ground, and get on to the Lord's ground, the ground of the Heavenly Man."

(D) PAUL AND ISRAEL

What was true of Peter had to be true of Paul. I think Paul was a long time in getting thoroughly off his own ground. He clung to Israel as long as he could. Other things there were that had quickly become clear, and his going out to the Gentiles had very largely moved him away even from this ground, but he was still clinging to it in measure. That vow, and that going up to Jerusalem which led him into such trouble, was all the fruit of his clinging to Israel, esteeming his brethren after the flesh above others. He did not easily let go. But when at length Paul let go of that ground, then he was able to write the letter to the Ephesians. The letter to the Ephesians is the glorious expression of heavenly ground having been reached in fulness. Is it not that? Ephesians deals with being in the heavenlies in Christ. It speaks of the stature of the fulness of Christ. The full-grown man is the Heavenly Man. At long last he has finally quitted his own ground, that of tradition, nature, birth, natural hope, and now, being on the ground of the Heavenly Man, he has such a fulness to pass on. He says—and it invests these words with such richness when you see what they represent of the position to which he him-self has come—"And put on the new man, that after God hath been created in righteousness and holiness of truth" (Ephesians iv. 24). On this heavenly ground, there can be neither Jew nor Greek. You must leave the ground of the Jew, leave the ground of the Greek. On this ground there can be neither circumcision nor uncircumcision. You have to leave both those grounds. On this ground there can be nei-ther barbarian nor Scythian, neither bondman nor freeman, but Christ is all, and in all. That is the ground of the Heavenly Man.

ALL NATURAL GROUND MUST BE FORSAKEN

In this dispensation God is not meeting Jews as Jews, and Gen-tiles as Gentiles, and a great many are making the mistake of think-ing that He is. His Word to the Jew is: "You must leave your Jewish ground, and stand before God, not as a Jew, but as a man, and until you take that ground God has nothing to say to you; you will not have any light whilst you persist in coming before God on your own ground." The same has to be said to everyone else. We have to leave our own ground in every way.

As that applies in these directions nationally, it applies in every other thing. Are you going to answer the Lord back: "But I am this or that, or something else"; or, "But I am not this or that." It is not what you are, but what the Son is, that is of account. Come on to His ground. The Lord will not meet you on the ground of what you are, whether it be good or bad; He will meet you on the ground of the Heavenly Man. Do you answer back, "I am so weak!" The Lord is not going to meet you on that ground; He will meet you on the ground of His Son. That is what the Holy Spirit means by such words as He speaks through Paul: "...be strengthened in the grace that is in Christ Jesus" (II Timothy ii. 1). God hears us exclaim. "But I am so weak, Lord!" But He does not pay any heed to what we mean to indicate by that confession, which is: "Come down on to the ground of my weakness and pick me up!" He says, "You forsake that ground, and come on to the ground of My Son, and you will find strength there." "I am so foolish, Lord!" The Lord says: "You will remain foolish until you get on to the ground of My Son, who is made unto you wisdom."

That applies all the way along. We take our own ground before the Lord and are surprised that the Lord does not lift us right out of our own ground and put us into a better position, but He never does. We shall stay there for ever, if that is our attitude. The Lord's word to us is: "Forsake your own ground and come on to My ground. I have provided a Heavenly Man who is full of all that you need; now come on to that ground." It does not matter what you are, or what you are not. There everything is adjusted and made good.

THE WITNESS OF THE TESTIMONIES TO THE TRUTH: (A) BAPTISM

This is the meaning of the testimonies of baptism and the laying on of hands, as mentioned in Hebrews vi. Those testimonies go together. Baptism is, on the one hand, leaving your own ground of nature, dying to your own ground and being buried. So far as your own natural ground is concerned, that is finished with: "Ye died...." You have parted from your own ground of nature. In your baptism, on the other hand, you were raised together with Christ, and you have come on to the ground of Christ, the Heavenly Man. "Having been buried with him in baptism, wherein ye were also raised with him through faith in the working of God, who raised him from the dead" (Colossians ii. 12). It is thus that the truth of which we have been speaking is set forth in Colossians. And the Apostle goes on to urge the recognition of it. "If ye died with Christ from the rudiments of the world, why, as though living in the world, do ye subject yourselves to ordinances?..." (Colossians ii. 20). Ye died! Ye died! You are now on other ground, the ground of the Heavenly Man. In resurrection you were raised together with Christ; seek, therefore, those things which are above.

May we just say here, lest some fall into a peril which we recognise in making such a statement, that amongst the things mentioned it says that you died to being under bondage to the Sabbath. That is quite true as a legal thing, as a part of a legal system imposed upon you; you have died to that, and you are no longer in bondage to that. But, mark you, we do not believe that a risen man, a spiritual man, will violate the principle of the Sabbath. We do not believe that a really spiritual man will do that. There is that portion of our time which is the Lord's portion, that which must be set aside for the Lord apart from all other things in the matter of time, that which must give the Lord His place and give a clear space for the Lord's things in our week. It is a settled law of a spiritual character that lies behind the ordinance of the Sabbath. I cannot believe for a moment that a man who is under the government of the Holy Spirit will treat every day alike, and turn the Sabbath day into a day of personal pleasure and gain. The Holy Spirit would check a spiritual man on such a matter, at the same time keeping him free from the legal Sabbath, so that he holds it unto God and not as a part of a legal religious system.

Now we say that in parenthesis to safeguard what has just been expressed against an unwarranted conclusion. "Oh, well, I can do as I like because I am not under the Law," someone will say. Oh no! Not at all! We can have the Holy Ghost now in resurrection, and on the ground of the Heavenly Man we shall be kept right by the Lord in these matters.

You see that baptism sets forth, on the one hand, our having forsaken our own ground of nature, through death, and, on the other hands, our having come on to the ground of the Heavenly Man in resurrection.

(B) THE LAYING ON OF HANDS

But then we come to the laying on of hands. That immediately follows baptism in the Scripture of Hebrews vi. What is the significance of the laying on of hands? It witnesses to our coming on to the ground of the corporate Heavenly Man, the one Body, so that in the laying on of hands there is the testimony borne between two or three, or more, by an act of identification, that we are not isolated units, but that we are a collective or corporate body, the corporate Heavenly Man. The ground of the Lord Himself was that of the one Body, that of the corporate Heavenly Man. There is no doubt that it is in that life of oneness in the Spirit, as the life of the Heavenly Man, that we find the greater fulnesses of Christ. There is always something more in two than in one. There is always something more of the Lord in relatedness than in isolation. The Lord indicates this very clearly when by the writer to the Hebrews He says: "Not forsaking the assembling of ourselves together, as the manner of some is, but exhorting one another: and so much the more, as ye see the day approaching" (Hebrews x. 25 KJV). Why should it be said "as ye see the day approaching"? Because it is the day of the fulness, the day of the consummation. Our coming together "so much the more" in view of that day makes possible the Lord's giving so much the more unto that final fulness. We need it so much the more as we get near the end, and near the beginning of "the day." The ground of the Heavenly Man, personal and corporate, is the ground that we have quite definitely to take.

In Christ, the Heavenly Man, everything lives. The ruling principle of the Heavenly Man is eternal life. Everything lives in Him. We have been saying that in Him the Word of God lives. On the ground of the Heavenly Man, the Word becomes alive. Get on to that ground and you will prove that things are really alive. Forsake your own ground and take His, and you will find life. Put it to the test if you like. If you keep your ground you will die, or you will remain in death. You say: "But, Lord, I am so weak!" Well, stay on that ground and see whether you do not die. "Lord, I am so foolish!" Well, stay there, and see how much life you enjoy. The realm of "what I am" is the realm of death. And even though it be the other kind of "I" that thinks itself to be something, that is, a certain self-satisfaction, self-fulness, it is death. The ground of "what I am," whatever it may be, is the ground of death. It is not the ground of the Heavenly Man. Get on to the ground of the Heavenly Man and you find life. Forsake your own ground and take His, and it will be life.

If you get upset, offended, and go off and sulk, and nurse your grievance, you will die. Are you expecting the Lord to come out to you there and intreat you: "Oh, do not be so upset, do not make so much of it!" The Lord will do nothing of the kind. He does not follow us out like that. He says to us: "You will have to forsake that ground and come back to My ground!" You will die out there! And you know it is not until you get over your huff and come back on to the Lord's ground that you begin to live again. Heavenly things are practical, not mythical. On any other ground than the Lord's ground there is death. If we separate ourselves, forsake that fellowship, that association which is our spiritual relationship in the will of God, we shall begin to lose, and become like Thomas. We are outside, losing ground, and our lives will become small, shrivelled, miserable. The Lord will not go out after a Thomas. The Lord never followed Thomas out. When the other disciples came together and Thomas was not with them, because he was offended, the Lord did not seek him out and say, "Come along, Thomas!" The Lord met them when they were together, and it was not until Thomas came in where they were that he met the Lord, and came into life, and came to see how silly he had been. Then Thomas fell down and said, "My Lord and my God." That is his confession to having been a fool.

If we separate ourselves and go off for any cause whatever, we shall die. The Lord will not come out to us in life. He will be saying to us all the time: "You must forsake that ground and come back again to where I can meet you, to where your life is." That is the ground of the corporate Heavenly Man. The Lord teach us the meaning of that.

THIRTEEN

THE CORPORATE EXPRESSION
OF THE HEAVENLY MAN

Reading: Ephesians iii. 17-21; iv. 1-10.

The fact that the Lord Jesus is the Heavenly Man is touched upon at various points in this reading. Here in chapter iv we have the statement that "He...ascended far above all the heavens..." while all that follows in the chapter is related to the present expression of the Heavenly Man as here in the world.

We have already noted this feature in John's Gospel; for we have there seen the Heavenly Man in person as both present here in the world and at the same time in Heaven. We now meet with it again in Ephesians, but this time in a wider sense; for here we have to do with the corporate expression of the same Heavenly Man in His Body, the Church.

These two are one, not merely by their relatedness, but by their very life; one in their resources, one in their mind, one in their consciousness, one in their nature, one in the laws of their life, one in their purpose, one in their method, one in their times. There is nothing which relates to them as the Heavenly Man in which they are not one. It is not just the oneness that springs from an understanding or an agreement, but that which is the result of being one in substance, one in essence.

Again, we are speaking of Christ as the Heavenly Man, and not of Him as God. In this corporate expression it is not a case of the Body acting for the Head, of the Church acting for the Lord. There is no independence nor separate responsibility. It is the Lord Himself continuing His own life and work in and through His Body; the whole is one Man. Not that the Lord has given up a personal identity and ceased to be a separate person, but as out from His very heavenly manhood He has given His own substance, His own constituents, His own life, to constitute a Body which is so one with Him, in this utter way, as to be part of Himself. That is the Body of Christ as set forth here. That is the Heavenly Man corporately expressed.

The Body, the Church, was never meant to be something in itself, but from eternity was always intended to be "the fulness of him that filleth all in all." Therefore it has no existence apart from Him, nor has it existence apart from God's purpose in Him. These facts, simple as they are in statement, are very profound, and very searching in their meaning. They govern and determine what the Church is. Nothing which bears the name "Church" (in the New Testament acceptation of that term) and is not the continuation of His Son in this universe, exists in the thought of God.

Now this involves several things, and these are presented in the chapter we have before us.

One Life in Christ

Firstly, this involves the one life that by the Holy Spirit is in all the members of Christ. "There is…one Spirit"; "Giving diligence to keep the unity of the Spirit…." There is the one life by the Holy Spirit. Only thus does Christ come to His fulness in His Body, does the Church fulfill the Divine thought for its existence, come to the Divine end.

We have already sought to see how the Heavenly Man in person was in every detail governed by the Spirit, inasmuch as upon such a government depended the fulfilment of the whole revelation of God concerning Him. All the Scriptures which had gone before pointed to Him, and waited for their fulfilment in Him, and He was to be the fulfilment of all those Scriptures to a detail. It would have been an impossible, overwhelming, crushing responsibility to have taken that on mentally, to have felt a consciousness every instant of His life that He was responsible for everything that was written in the Scriptures.

To have had that on His mind would have been an intolerable burden impossible of bearing. He would have been the most introspective person that had ever lived. Every moment He would have been asking: "Am I doing the right thing? Am I doing it in the right way? Am I doing what I ought to be doing according to that Book, that standard?" But His life, being governed by the anointing, being under the control of the Spirit, meant that He spontaneously, and by the inward consciousness that was His through the Holy Spirit as to what was, and what was not, the mind of God, did fulfil the whole revelation.

Now what was true of Him personally has to be true of Him in the corporate sense. Here is a revelation concerning Jesus Christ which has come out of the eternal counsels of God, a revelation of vast meaning, a destiny, a great spiritual, heavenly system summed up in Him, and which is to be expressed, to be wrought out, to be realised in Him corporately as in Him personally. But how is it possible for us to fulfil it, to realise it, to attain unto it; for it to have its fulfilment and its expression in us? Only on the basis of the one life by Holy Spirit in all. That is what gives force to the exhortation in this very letter to "...be filled with the Spirit." That gives the real meaning and value to the whole teaching concerning the Holy Spirit— the receiving of the Spirit, walking in the Spirit, being led by the Spirit—because only so can that which has been produced by the mind of God, concerning His Son, and which is to have its full realisation in the Body of Christ, be reached. How necessary, then, for us all to live in the Spirit. It is not enough that some of us should live in the Spirit; it is important that all should do so, and that none should walk after the flesh.

AN INTER-RELATED AND INTER-DEPENDENT LIFE

The second thing, which is really a part of the same truths, but with perhaps a rather closer application of it, is the need for a recognition of, and diligence to keep, an inter-related and inter-dependent life. It is something to be recognised first of all, to be taken account of, and then something we are to be diligent to maintain. That is to say, all the members of Christ are related; there is an inter-relationship. We are not so many separate parts, fragments, individuals, we are all related; and not only so, but we are all dependent on one another. For God's end, for God's purpose, we cannot do without one another. On any level other than that we might be able to do without one another. If we were living on any natural level, we could perhaps say of some people, that we could do without them, but when we come into the light of God's purpose, then we are governed by an inter-dependence. We find that we need one another, that we are dependent upon one another, in respect of God's fulness. Of this fact we have a clear indication in the words "strong to apprehend *with all the saints.*" We cannot apprehend apart from the rest. No one of us will ever be able to apprehend the whole. We need the strength of all saints to apprehend with all saints.

This is not only a statement of fact, but a truth by which we are immediately put to the test. Do we say: "Well, we have seen the Body of Christ, we have seen the Church!" As to whether we have seen that aright, will be proved by whether we realise our inter-dependence. If any one of us should ever take the attitude that we can dispense with another member of Christ, or be of that spirit, such a one has not truly seen the Body of Christ. Maybe there has been a seeing of something, but not the Body of Christ; it has not been seen that this Body is to be the fulness of Christ. For that fulness all saints are needed. The Lord Jesus in His own way, His own parabolic way, was putting His finger upon principles and laws all the time—"See that ye despise not one of these little ones..." (Matthew xviii. 10); "...Inasmuch as ye did it not unto one of these least..." (Matthew xxv. 45). This is not just a community kind of thing, a fraternity; we are face to face with a law, when it is said that it will take all saints to come to, and to express, His fulness. If we have seen the Body of Christ we must have seen the inter-relatedness and the inter-dependence of all members, and must be living on the basis that the Body is one.

The Apostle exhorts to diligence in relation to that. We must recognise that the Body is one, and then give diligence to keep the unity of the Spirit. I expect the Apostle, by the time he wrote his letter, well knew how much diligence that required. He was beginning to see how easy it was for Christians to dispense with one another, to take the attitude that they could do without one another, or without certain ones at any rate; how easy it was for them to fall apart, to take a careless attitude, to be anything but diligent in keeping the unity.

This maintaining of the unity is a positive thing. It represents a being on full stretch for something. It is not just a case of our desiring it, wanting it, of our considering it to be the best thing and even necessary, but of our applying it. It takes application to give diligence to keep the unity of the Spirit.

This is what is meant by being "renewed in the spirit of your mind," which, again, is unto the putting on of the "new man," the corporate Heavenly Man. Thus in the passage before us, the practical exhortation immediately follows: "Wherefore, putting away falsehood, speak ye truth each one with his neighbor: for we are members one of another" (Ephesians iv. 25). The renewing of the spirit of the mind works out in each one speaking truth with his neighbour, in the putting away of all falsehood. Why tell yourself a lie? We would not do that deliberately. What would be the point in my telling myself something that is not true? What would be the sense of my left hand doing my right hand an injury, seeing that ultimately both must suffer? Similarly "we are members one of another." In the other mind, the mind of the old man, which is mentioned here, there is a lack of this sense of corporate life, this inter-dependence, this inter-relationship, where it is recognised that everyone is necessary, indispensable. You can put people off in that realm; you can get rid of them, can gain your end, gain an advantage by just suspending the truth. But here we are dealing with one entity, and that entity must not be conflicting, must not be different things but one thing. We must be renewed in the spirit of our mind by putting on this new corporate Heavenly Man.

These verses are worth our noting again in the light of what we are saying:

"If so be that ye heard him, and were taught in him, even
as truth is in Jesus: that ye put away, as concerning your
former manner of life, the old man, that waxeth corrupt
after the lusts of deceit; and that ye be renewed in the
spirit of your mind, and put on the new man, that after
God hath been created in righteousness and holiness of

truth. Wherefore, putting away falsehood, speak ye truth
each one with his neighbor: for we are members one of
another" (Ephesians iv. 21-25).

That is the new mind of the "new man," which is renewed in the spirit on the principle, the law, the reality of inter-relatedness and inter-
dependence.

I need you; you are indispensable to me. I can never realise my
destiny, the purpose of my being, apart from you. What, then, is the
point in my telling you lies? If there is someone without whom our
destiny, the purpose of our being, our whole objective is impossible,
is lost, and, in the face of such a fact, a deceptive, lying relationship,
what a contradiction! That is the force of the words here. "We are
members one of another," therefore we must have a one mind; and
speaking truth one with another is a mark of the "new man," the
Heavenly Man who has only one mind. Lies all speak of contrary
minds.

GIFTS IN CHRIST

The third thing that this implies is that for the progressive realisation and expression of this Heavenly Man in time and in eternity,
the heavenly Head has given gifts.

"...When he ascended on high, he led captivity captive,
And gave gifts unto men. (...He that descended is the
same also that ascended far above all the heavens, that
he might fill all things.)" (Ephesians iv. 8-10).

There is the Heavenly Man in person as the heavenly Head, giving
gifts among men for the progressive realisation and expression of
Himself as the corporate Heavenly Man.

Now we must break that up and look at this parenthesis in verses 9 and 10. It carries with it this fact that He descended before He
ascended. He did not have His beginnings here. Of course we know
that, but this is the argument of the Apostle; His origin was not here.
By His ascending it is to be understood that He first descended.
There is the Heavenly Man coming down and being here among men,
the Heavenly Man in incarnation; He came down out of Heaven.

Having descended, He ascended, that He might fill all things. The whole universe is to be filled with the Heavenly Man.

Now you have to get that background before you can understand and appreciate what follows about these gifts. In relation to that filling of all things by the Heavenly Man, there is to be the increase of the Body. This chapter is all of a piece. Christ is not here as separated from His Body. Here the Heavenly Man in person and the corporate Heavenly Man are brought together as one in purpose. Earlier in the letter the Apostle has shown how before times eternal, in the thought of God, this Heavenly Man has come out of Heaven to be found here, but whilst here, is still in Heaven. Now He personally is to be the universal fulness, and that fulness is to be by the Church: "...glory in the church and in Christ Jesus unto all generations [unto the ages of the ages]...." In relation to that universal filling there is to be this increase of the Body: "...in whom each several building, fitly framed together, *groweth* into a holy temple in the Lord" (Ephesians ii. 21). In the letter to the Colossians there is a very similar word:

"And not holding fast the Head, from whom all the body, being supplied and knit together through the joints and bands, increasing with the increase of God" (Colossians ii. 19).

He is to fill all things by His Body, which is His fulness. Then the Body must grow, the Body must make increase, the Body must add to its stature, until it comes to the full measure of Christ. Now with a view to this increase, the heavenly gifts are given by the Heavenly Man to this heavenly Body.

Then I want you to notice another thing. These gifts are themselves a measure of Christ: "But unto each one of us was the grace given according to the measure of the gift of Christ" (Ephesians iv. 7). The gifts are a measure of Christ, and therefore they are all intended to produce the fulness of Christ, to lead to that fulness. In their own way they represent a fulness of Christ ministered in the Body. They are to make up the full measure.

Having seen that, we are able to look at the gifts mentioned.

Authority in Christ

"And he gave some, apostles…" (KJV). (It does not say "to be" apostles.) Then we need to know what the apostle represents as a measure of Christ. What is his value in bringing the fulness of Christ by way of the Body, the Church, the corporate Heavenly Man? It is impressive to recognise that the apostle stands first on account of the value associated with the apostle. What are apostles? There is one word which expresses the meaning of apostles, and that word is "authority." Authority comes first.

We know that grammatically speaking the word means "one sent." But look again to see its signification in the Word of God. Take the word wherever you find it and see what is in it. Look, for example, at the parable of the house-holder who planted a vineyard. He sent unto them his servants to receive of the fruit. They came with his authority, and the wicked husbandmen, in slaying the servants, wholly repudiated the master's authority. You see, the application to Israel there is so piercing. The point of the parable is that they were refusing to acknowledge the authority of God in Christ. When the owner of the vineyard comes himself to deal with the situation he will miserably destroy the husbandmen. On what ground will he do this? Because he did not get his own personal gratification in the fruits? No! Because they had refused to recognise his authority in his son—"…he sent unto them his son…." Wherever you find the "sent" of the Lord, you find the authority of the Lord. That is an apostle.

As you carefully consider the matter of apostleship, you will see that everything that constituted an apostle represented what made for authority. An apostle was a specially constituted servant of the Lord. There was a very rigid Law governing apostleship (so far as the Twelve were concerned), that an apostle must have seen the Lord in resurrection. He could not be an apostle if the Lord had not appeared unto him, for he had not had first-hand knowledge of the risen Lord. That first-hand knowledge of the risen Lord invested him with an authority. It was a matter of the Lord having Himself appeared unto him.

If you turn to the letter to the Hebrews you will find that the Lord Jesus is spoken of as God's Apostle and High Priest. The very phrase at once carries us back in thought to the writings of Moses, and we mark how it combines what God has set forth in Moses and Aaron respectively. Moses as the apostle, and Aaron as the high priest, represent two aspects of the Lord Jesus. Moses represents authority. From the beginning of God's using of Moses, right to the end, Moses represented the authority of God. The rod which was Moses' rod, became the rod of God, and by that rod the authority of God was displayed. The authority of God was so much vested in him that God was able to say to him, regarding Aaron, "...thou shalt be to him as God" (Exodus iv. 16).

We see later how that worked out. When there were those who tried to displace Moses, or tried to take an equal place with him, see how the authority found expression. Moses never had to fight for his position. When the dispute arose touching his position, being the meekest of men, he just said to the Lord, in effect: "Lord, am I here by Your authority, or am I not? Have I grasped this position? Have I sought authority, or have You put me here with it? I count on You to let it be known whether my position is of my own taking, or whether of Your appointing." The Lord called the people to the door of the tabernacle and took up the case of Moses, and you know what happened. It was because of what he represented as an apostle.

"...All authority hath been given unto me in heaven and on earth. Go ye therefore..." (Matthew xxviii. 18, 19). Thus an apostle is one who stands in Divine authority for the setting up, and the carrying on, of the Divine testimony. You can see that in Moses. The Lord appeared unto Moses and spake with him face to face. No one else came into that realm. Even though they came up into the Mount, they did not come into exactly the same place as Moses. It was with Moses that the Lord communed and spake as a man speaks to his friend, face to face. Then for ever after, the one thing that governs Israel is this: "...as Jehovah spake unto Moses...." At the end of the constituting of the tabernacle, there is a whole chapter in which some seven or eight times this one phrase occurs:...as Jehovah commanded Moses." It speaks of authoritative government by what had come in through Moses, God's apostle. Well, in that authority he set up the testimony, and maintained it; the authority was his to that end.

Or, again, take the Apostle Paul, who perhaps above all others stands out as an apostle, and you see that his commission and his authority was, first of all, for the setting up of the testimony everywhere, and then for the maintaining of the testimony. He says to the Corinthians that, if he comes to them in the authority that he has received, it will go ill with some of them, because he is invested with this authority to maintain the testimony in purity.

Now what does this say to us? It is the Lord! This is the factor of Christ's heavenly authority in the corporate Heavenly Man. That may be administered through individuals. The point is that it is a feature of the Heavenly Man, and is active in the Church. We are face to face with the fact that Christ in His heavenly authority is in the Church for the setting up of His testimony, and the maintaining of it. Where the Lord's testimony is by the Holy Ghost, there the authority of the Lord is, and people have to reckon with that.

Of course, while we have to take these things to heart in our own personal lives, we are saying them as to those who have to instruct others. As the Lord's servants, you cannot have too clear a recognition of how definite is this operation of the authority of Christ in His Body. None can anywhere come into relationship with that corporate expression of Christ, which is constituted by the Holy Ghost, without becoming responsible for the Lord's testimony which is there, and if you violate it you suffer. You cannot just attach yourself, and escape the implications. If you make a breach of the testimony, of the oneness of the Body of Christ, when you have been brought into real touch with it, and do not put that right, you will die. You may die physically. You may have a tragic end. You will undoubtedly go through sufferings and chastening; because you have not become a member of a movement, something merely of man; you have come into the place where the custodianship of eternal purpose is invested in the Holy Ghost working in the spirit of apostleship, and the authority of Christ is there. This is the precise meaning of those searching words in the first letter to the Corinthians: "For this cause many among you are weak and sickly, and not a few sleep," and "not discerning the Lord's body" (see I Corinthians xi. 29, 30). You have come into a realm where things are not to be taken as mere doctrine, as an organisation, as something of man with which you can do as you like; you have to come to the place where the authority of Christ is an operating reality. It is a terrible thing to get into the House of God if you are not of a mind to become suitably conformed.

That is one side, and a terrible side. But there is another side that makes for heart rest and assurance for those who carry extra responsibility in the house of God, where it is possible to say: "Well, we have not to bear the full responsibility that properly is in the hands of the Holy Ghost, in the authority of Christ, to meet that which is contrary to the truth, and to the law of the house of God." We need not be anxious, in that sense, because it is our responsibility. The heavenly Lord has put a functioning of His authority in the Church. There may be a disputing of that authority in the vessel. Hell may dispute, as at Philippi, or at Ephesus, or many another place, and may show its hands in vehement antagonism and resistance. But what is the issue? Every time the authority of Christ triumphs.

The establishment of the testimony throughout the Roman Empire through the Apostle Paul, is a marvelous manifestation of the supreme Lordship of Jesus Christ over all powers. It is not just a case of getting the better of man's mentality, of overcoming prejudice and difficulties amongst men; it is the conquest of the evil force of hell. Cosmic forces are beaten and broken when the testimony is established through an apostle. It is the fact of Christ's heavenly authority in the Body, by the Spirit. Christ truly expressed in the assembly really cannot be set aside without suffering.

THE MIND OF GOD IN CHRIST

Now what are the prophets in the assembly? In a word, the prophet is the instrument for the expression of the mind of the Lord, and this is usually set over against the expression of the mind of man. Of very great moment is the injunction we have noted already, "...be renewed in the spirit of your mind...." Because, in the corporate Heavenly Man, the Body, the mind of the Lord is to predominate, to operate, to be supreme. The Lord's mind is the only mind in this "new man," this Heavenly Man. You must be renewed in the spirit of your mind, if you are to come to the Lord's mind. The Lord's mind comes through an instrument called a prophet. He is the interpreter of the mind of the Lord. He brings into the Body the knowledge of the mind of the Lord. That, as we have said, involves the setting aside of the mind of man.

We are thinking, of course, of how the Old Testament prophets are a source of confirmation of what we have just said; for if you examine the point, you will find that they come before the people in relation to the rights of God in His House. Those rights were being set aside by His people. The mind of man was taking the place of the mind of God, and that worked out usually to very great evil, so that before long the very rights of God were denied Him in His own House, amongst His own people.

Take Elijah as an example. Elijah stands out pre-eminently amongst the prophets in relation to the rights of God, and Carmel is the great crisis as to Baal's rights and God's rights in Israel. Elijah is the instrument for establishing the rights of God in an utter way, unto the complete destruction of that other mind, represented in the prophets of Baal. Those rights are expressed in terms of God's mind for His people, and so all the prophets bring in the mind of God, interpret it, keep the mind of God before God's people, and do battle in relation to it, that God shall have His place, have things according to His mind.

This, again, is a functioning of the Heavenly Man in His Body, to keep things according to the mind of God. We are not thinking, at the moment, particularly of people whom we may think to call prophets amongst us. We are not thinking of office, but of function. Vital functioning is what is before us, and anyone who is anointed and endowed by the Holy Spirit to keep God's thoughts clear in the midst of His people, to make His people know the mind of God, so that God gets His place and His rights, and all other minds are set aside, is fulfilling the ministry of a prophet. We are so apt to start at the other end, with the technical line of things, that of appointing prophets. Let us look at the function, not the man, and let us see that it is Christ who is the Prophet, and that in this character He ministers through some whom He gives for the expression of the Divine mind as in Himself. It is quite possible to combine these functions in one individual.

THE HEART OF GOD IN CHRIST

Now what are the evangelists? In a word, the evangelist is the one to make God known through the Gospel, to disclose the heart of God in grace, and the function of the evangelist is to secure material for the expression of the Heavenly Man corporately. Thus we begin with authority in Christ, Christ in the place of supreme authority far above all heavens. Then we have the mind of God in Christ. Here we have the heart of God in Christ. The Gospel of grace is to secure increase by gathering material for the corporate Heavenly Man.

RESOURCES OF GOD IN CHRIST

We now come to the pastors and teachers. These two are brought together. The material is being gathered, the corporate Heavenly Man is being progressively brought into being and coming to His eternal completeness. Now while the material is being gathered, and the corporate Heavenly Man is being progressively brought together, the next need is for pastors and teachers, and the function here is that of the adjustment and fitting of that Heavenly Man. Adjustment is brought about by teaching, by instruction. The purpose of the instruction is to adjust us, to bring us into our place, into our right relationship, to bring us into an understanding of Christ, of our relationship to Him, and of our relationship to one another in Him. The instruction has to do with such matters as the believer's resources in Christ, and all that is signified by the Heavenly Man. This is the work of the teacher. The pastor is one whose function is to fit, to shepherd, to nurture. Building up by right adjustment to revealed truth is what we have here.

But all does not end there. The apostle, the prophet, the evangelist, the pastor and teacher, are given in order that the corporate Heavenly Man, deriving the values of these functions, shall itself minister to its mutual building up; for the making complete of the saints unto the work of the ministry, unto the building up of the Body of Christ. Mutual building up, mutual ministry, is to result from these gifts. Because we are receiving the benefits of this ministration in Christ to us, we have to make those benefits a mutual ministration, so that the Body builds itself up, increases with the increase of God, each separate part in due measure making increase.

If this sounds like technique to you, may we urge you to get away from teaching, and anything like a system of truth, and get the Lord in view. Keep the Lord Himself in view, and see that the one thing which governs all is Christ's coming into ever greater fulness of life and expression in this universe by means of the Church which is His Body.

FOURTEEN

I. Judas—The Indwelling of Satan in Its Outworking; II. The Heavenly Man—The Indwelling of God

Reading: John xiii. 21-33; Ephesians iii. 17-19; Colossians i. 25-27.

We are to view the Lord Jesus in relation to the first Adam, and all that came in through that which happened with the first Adam in his fall, not only as this has reference to man and his condition, but to all that which Adam's act of disobedience let into this universe, and into this world. That act of disobedience opened the door at which the forces of evil were standing, waiting for access. Adam was that door. They could never have got in but for Adam, but he opened the door by his disobedience, and the forces of evil rushed into God's creation, and took up a position of great strength, to bring about in it a state of things contrary to God, and that in the most powerful and terrible way. To all of that, to the powers themselves, and the state brought about through their being let in, and all the consequences thereof, the Lord Jesus was, and is, God's answer. But there was a secret about Him, a secret which spiritual intelligences alone could really discern, and this was that God was in Him. He was a Man, but He was far more than that; He was God. In these meditations our concern has been with what the Lord Jesus is as Son of Man, God's Man, the Heavenly Man, in whom God was, and is. That secret, that mystery hidden from the ages, hidden from men, is the greatest factor to be reckoned with.

So far as the enemy was concerned, his main objective with the Lord Jesus was to seek to get in between Him and that Divine relationship; to drive a wedge in and in some way to get Him to move on a ground apart from that inner, deepest reality of the Father. The meaning of the temptations in the wilderness is that they were an attempt to drive that wedge in between, to get Him to act apart from the Father, to move on His own human ground. The enemy knew quite well that, if only he could succeed in getting Him to do that, he would accomplish with the last Adam what he had accomplished with the first, and would have re-established his dominion and again gained the mastery. The secret of Christ's victory was that He was so one with the Father, that in everything He was governed by the Father within, dwelling in Him. The life of the Heavenly Man, the Son of Man, again and again bids us heed the question that once came from His own lips: "Believest thou not that I am in the Father, and the Father in me...?" (John xiv. 10). It was on that basis that He lived His life and met the enemy, and because He remained on that basis the enemy was incapable of destroying Him.

Many times attempts were made by the Devil to destroy Him, both directly and through men, but it was impossible while He remained on that basis, and this He did right to the end, and triumphed because of that inward relationship, that upon which He was living deliberately, consciously, persistently: the Father was in Him, and He and the Father were one; He dwelt in the Father, and the Father dwelt in Him.

But—and this is one of the main points that we want the Lord to show us at this time—that was the great secret, the wonderful secret which men could not read; for He Himself said, "...no one knoweth who the Son is, save the Father..." (Luke x. 22). John, writing his epistle long years after, said, "...the world knoweth us not, because it knew him not" (I John iii. 1). The world knew Him not. In His own prayer recorded by John, we have these words: "O righteous Father, the world knew thee not, but I knew thee..." (John xvii. 25). It was on the basis of the secret relationship that there was to be a glorifying of Him. The glorifying of the Lord Jesus was bound up with that secret.

Now we want to know what the glorifying of the Son is, the glorifying of the Heavenly Man. We will again first take up the question in relation to the Heavenly Man in person, and then see how the same thing applies to the corporate Heavenly Man.

"When therefore he was gone out, Jesus saith, Now is the
Son of man glorified, and God is glorified in him; and
God shall glorify him in himself, and straightway shall
he glorify him" (John xiii. 31, 32).

We need not be concerned for the moment with the form of the statement. It sounds a little involved and difficult, but let us take the central comprehensive statement: "Now is the Son of man glorified, and God is glorified in him...." It is upon the word "now" that everything hangs, and the Lord Jesus put into that little word a tremendous meaning. To what does that word relate? "When therefore he [Judas] was gone out, Jesus saith, *Now* is the Son of Man glorified."

THE REJECTED NATURAL MAN

I confess that Judas was a problem to me for many years, but I think I am getting near the truth about him, and this passage seems to give us the clue. The problem, of course, has its occasion in the statement of the Lord Jesus that He knew whom He had chosen: "Did not I choose you the twelve, and one of you is a devil?" (John vi. 70). He chose Judas and brought him into association with Himself, in such a way that he had all the advantages of the others and all the facilities that were theirs; all the benefits of the others were open to him. There is no trace of partiality. He has placed Judas apparently upon exactly the same footing, excluding him from nothing which was open to the rest, all deliberately, consciously, knowing what He was doing, and knowing all the time what Judas was. Then all finally heads up to this statement, "Now is the Son of man glorified...."

I do not know how best to put it, and wish I had language and wisdom to express this, that would capture your hearts as it has captured mine; for I am inwardly glorying in what is brought to us here.

To begin with, this represents the full development of man under the kindness of God: "…for he maketh his sun to rise on the evil and the good, and sendeth rain on the just and the unjust" (Matthew v. 45). God has shown no partiality amongst men. He has made it possible for all men to enjoy His benefits. He has shown unbelieving, God-less, rebellious men great kindness. He has not discriminated. All men may know His kindness and His goodness. Man is thus represented in Judas, who in this figurative way is here set in relation to the Lord, so that what is available to those who are really the Lord's is available to him; he can come into it, it is open to him. The Lord has not shown any partiality. Yet man, living under the beneficent, merciful and gracious will, purpose, thought, and desire of God, can develop to this.

Let us seek to explain that. Man has been tried under every condition from the beginning. First of all he was tried under innocence. How did he behave? He failed. Then in his fallen state he was tried again, without law. How did he get on? He failed again. Then he was tried under law, but failed as before. Man has failed under every condition. He has been tried by God in every state and appointment, and has utterly failed. The end has always been a tragedy. No matter what attitude God takes toward man, in himself he is a failure and will work out to the most dreadful tragedy.

Look at Israel. What is the attitude of the Lord toward Israel? How marvellous is the way the Lord dealt with Israel. Look at the patience of God with Israel, the kindness of God with Israel, the ground upon which Israel was set before Him. In effect, God said: "You have only to show something of faithfulness to Me and you will immediately receive blessing." Some of us have wished we could get blessing as instantly as Israel did when they were true to the Lord. They were subjects of such special care, but they failed. Their condition and treatment is figuratively set forth in the unprofitable fig-tree, that bore no fruit in spite of years of care. Justice demanded that it be cut down without delay, but still further opportunity is given: "Let us dig about it and dung it this year also." Let us show kindness for another year! But it is just as big a failure. So man, tried under every condition, brought into touch with the beneficent will of God, is yet a failure.

Judas gathers up man, man to whom is open all that God has, man who is brought into touch with all the good and perfect will of God, and yet in himself the most awful failure; for this man, when he comes to his fulness, will betray his Lord, he is so hopeless. Man in himself, even though the mercies of God may go out to him, will arrive at this. This is a fearful end. "Yea, mine own familiar friend…who did eat of my bread," says the Psalmist, "hath lifted up his heel against me" (Psalm xli. 9). Thus will this man do amidst the very wealth of the grace of God.

Here is Judas representing one who has been brought into touch with the Lord, and to whom all the blessings are open that are open to the rest of the Lord's own, and this is how he turns out. It is a picture of man in himself. Is it not true? The full development of old Adam, of the first Adam, in whom God does not dwell, is here shown to us. Just at the point where this man is surrounded with all the advantages, all the facilities, all the blessings, all the opportunity, all that could have been his, just at that point he goes out to betray his Lord: "…and it was night" (John xiii. 30). There is a world of meaning in that.

THE HEAVENLY MAN OF GOD'S ELECTION

Instantly that man has gone out the Lord Jesus says, "Now is the Son of man glorified…." What does this mean? This is God's answer to all that. God has another Man, whose path is to be wholly different from that tragedy, that dark calamity, a Son of Man who can be glorified. God has prepared His own Man to take the place of this other man, as soon as he has reached his end: and what an evil end it is! Do you see what is signified in the end of Judas? When he goes out God brings in His Man who can be glorified.

Do you see why the Lord Jesus chose Judas? Do you see why it is that when he was gone out Jesus said, "Now is the Son of man glorified"? There is the one who represents the Adam man and what he comes to in spite of all God's grace and mercy which is at his command. Until there is something in him other than himself, that is what he comes to. And just when that nature, that man, that race is seen in its full awfulness, its full outworking, lifting its heel in treachery against the God of all grace; just when that man reaching fulness goes out into the dark, the eternal night, God begins His new day by bringing in His new Man to take his place.

What is the secret? What kind of man will be glorified? We have seen the man who cannot be glorified, who goes out into the darkness. What kind of man is he who can be glorified? What is the principle and secret of His glorifying? It is that God is in him. What is the glorifying of the Lord Jesus? It is the breaking forth and manifesting of the Father in Him, of that secret which makes Him other than the type represented by Judas. The hope of glory in His case, the certainty of glory, was the Father dwelling in Him. "Now is the Son of man glorified, and God is glorified in him." That is a full-orbed statement about the glorifying of the Son of Man. It is remarkable that this statement should be found in the Gospel by John, in which the Lord Jesus is pre-eminently set forth as the Son of God.

THE GLORIFYING OF THE CORPORATE HEAVENLY MAN

Now, of course, we come to feel the benefit and the power of this, when it is transferred from the personal Heavenly Man to the corporate Heavenly Man. So the Apostle says: "That Christ may dwell in your hearts through faith…" (Ephesians iii. 17); "…Christ in you, the hope of glory…" (Colossians i. 27). We read at the beginning of the letter to the Ephesians that we are "…a habitation of God in the Spirit" (ii. 22). What does this mean in its value and out-working? This Body, so created and living upon that fact, is as indestructible as Christ Himself, is as certain of victory as was Christ. On the principle that Christ dwells in the heart by faith, this Body can enter into wrestling with principalities and powers, world rulers of this darkness, spiritual hosts of wickedness in the heavenlies, and come out victor on the field.

What is the secret of the glorifying of the Church, His Body, the corporate Man, and what is the nature of the glorifying? It is the same thing. It is the manifestation of the secret, the coming out from secrecy into open display of that which is true, of Christ within. During the course of this dispensation, the secret is in the Church, in the members of Christ, but "...the world knoweth us not, because it knew him not" (I John iii. 1). Looked at from the outside we are very little different from any other people in the world. Yet the secret is there, and this secret means that if you touch that one, or that church, you touch God. "Saul, Saul, why persecutest thou me?" said the Lord, when Saul was touching His members. He is in His members. You have to reckon with Him. They are indestructible, they cannot be destroyed. We are not talking about the destroying of the body. The true Church is an indestructible entity. When Satan has done his worst, that Church will still stand triumphant, and will abide for ever, when he and all his shall have been banished from the universe.

At the end of this dispensation which has held this hidden secret, there will be an unveiling of the Christ in His Church, when it appears with Him in glory, and it will be glorified on the same principle as that on which He was glorified.

THE ESSENTIAL BASIS OF THE BELIEVER'S EVERY-DAY LIFE

Now, there is something that we have to take to our own hearts out of these inclusive factors. We have to live all the time on this basis that we have set forth, and as we do so the enemy's power is absolutely rendered nil. Our trouble is that we do not live upon this basis. We live so much upon ourselves. We live upon our own feelings, our own conditions, our own state, anything and everything that is ourselves, and because we do that we are simply played with by the Devil. When we get into our own mood, what a mess he makes of us. When we get into our own feelings, or our own thoughts, what havoc there is. Anything that is ourselves, if we get into that, and live on that, will give the enemy an opportunity to do as he likes. Whenever believers get down into themselves, on to the ground of what they are, if it is only for a moment, they begin to lose their balance, their poise, their rest, their peace, their joy, and they are tossed about of the Devil at his will. They may come to the place where they even wonder whether they are saved. Let us remember that the part of us which still belongs to the fallen creation, and will not survive, is the playground of the enemy, and it is of no use our trying to make it survive.

We have, for instance, a physical life. Within the compass of this natural, physical life as a part of the old creation, anything is possible. Mental darkness is possible. The upsetting of our nervous system can be of such a kind as to make us feel that hell rages in our very being. Anything is possible of moods, and feelings, and sensations, or of utter deadness and numbness, and if we live in that realm the Devil plays havoc. He encamps upon such things at once, if we take our natural condition as the criterion. There is no hope of glory in that natural realm.

How is the enemy to be defeated, to be nullified, to be robbed of his power? On the same principle as in the life of the Lord Jesus, by our living on the Father. We must live on the indwelling Christ. Our attitude will have to be continually toward the Lord: "Lord, in me Thou art other than I am; Thou art not what I am; Thou art other than this mood, than this feeling, than this absence of feeling; Thou art other than all these thoughts, other than I am! I am dead, so far as my feelings are concerned, but Thou art other than that, Thou art living! I am feeling dark, Thou art the light, and Thou art in me! This is me, this is not the Lord!" If only you and I will learn steadily (it will take time, it will be progressive) to live on in Christ, on what He is, on the fact that He is other than we are—not upon our experience of this, but the naked fact that He is within us—if we will steadily learn to live on that basis, by that great Divine reality, then the enemy has nothing in us. The Lord Jesus was able to say, "...the prince of the world cometh: and he hath nothing in me..." (John xiv. 30). What was the adversary looking for? He was looking for the Lord Jesus to be living somewhere in Himself, consulting His own feelings, leaning to His own understanding, following His own judgments, His own will. If we could have caught Him there, he would have had something in Him and disturbed the balance of His life. The Lord Jesus was able to say, "...I live because of the Father..." (John vi. 57); "I live by the Father, not on what I am." He could say that as a perfect, sinless being, living none the less in dependence upon the Father all the time. Of this we have His own testimony:

"...The Son can do nothing of himself..." (John v. 19); "...the words that I say unto you I speak not from myself: but the Father abiding in me doeth his works" (John xiv. 10). He lived all the time on the basis of the Father dwelling within, and because of that the enemy had no ground whatever.

This is the lesson of life for us. For any glory within now, or for any hope of glory in the great day of the manifestation, the sole ground of expectation must be Christ in us; because the glory is simply the manifestation of the Father within.

The Church, a Mystery of a Divine Indwelling

Now concerning the corporate expression of this Heavenly Man, in the letter to the Ephesians the Apostle tells us that something is going on in the unseen, the purpose of which is stated thus: "...that now unto the principalities and the powers in the heavenly places might be made known through the church the manifold wisdom of God" (Ephesians iii. 10). I wonder what that means? I do not know altogether, but I think I can see something of what it means. I believe the unseen intelligences are watching to see how they can get an advantage. They are watching with all their cunning, their diabolical wit and wisdom and ingenuity, with all their superhuman intelligence, to see how they can get an advantage, how they can make a stroke, if by any means they can get the upper hand of this baffling creation, the Church. Unto the principalities and powers the manifold wisdom of God is being made known by the Church. How is this being accomplished? A clause from a verse in the first letter to Timothy will, I think, help us towards the answer. "And without controversy great is the mystery of godliness; He who was manifested in the flesh, justified in the spirit, seen of angels, preached among the nations, believed on in the world, received up in glory" (iii. 16). A part of the mystery here spoken of is this somewhat obscure statement that He was "seen of angels." I cannot be satisfied with the thought that this just means that the heavenly angels saw Him, either when He was in the flesh, or after His resurrection. This seems to say to my heart (of course I cannot prove it, but I am comparing Scripture with Scripture, and taking into account that it is the Holy Spirit who has disclosed this fact and brought it to our knowledge) that these other angels, these spiritual intelligences who had watched for a chance against His life, seeking an advantage, using their cunning, saw now who He was, saw the full meaning of His being, and why they had never succeeded in compassing their design, but had been compelled to learn their impotence regarding Him. They know now, because the secret is out. This Man is other than the first Adam; He is different from the first Adam! They got their chance with the first Adam and they took it, and into that race they brought the diabolical wisdom of which the Apostle says, "This wisdom is...devilish [demoniacal]" (James iii. 15).

These intelligences had been waiting for an opportunity to bring in their wisdom in this other Adam, this last Adam, and they could not get it. They were beaten and defeated at every point, and now the secret is out, and they see One over whom they could gain no advantage. Why was this? Because of the Father dwelling in Him. It is to this same truth that Paul refers when he says that Christ crucified, so far from being the wisdom of this world, is the wisdom of God. His wisdom far transcends the wisdom of this world, which in its nature is demoniacal. God is still further displaying His manifold wisdom to principalities and powers through the Church, the Body of Christ, the corporate Heavenly Man. How is this being accomplished? By the mystery of Christ within, defeating their every plan, their every scheme, by the great reality of the indwelling Lord whose wisdom is so much greater than theirs.

Oh that we could live upon the great reality, the great essential, the great secret of the very being of the Church according to God's mind, that basic secret of Christ within; not upon what we are at any time, but what Christ is. If you take that position you will be in a position of wisdom that outwits all the cunning of the Devil, and outmatches all his power.

Put it to the test; for it is open to practical proof at any time. If when you are next feeling desperately bad and hopeless and full of evil in yourself, as though all that you had believed in no longer held water and everything had gone to pieces, and all the sensations are upon you that it is possible for one to have, till you could well believe that you are lost; if, when this is so, you will take the position that it is all to do with your poor, broken down creation, and that Christ in you is other than that, and by faith stand on Him, the Devil's power is destroyed, his wisdom is outwitted, and there is glory. That is the lesson we have to learn. Christ in you, and in the Church as the habitation of God through the Spirit, is the symbol of glory, of victory, of power and wisdom. Blessed be God, there are seasons when this reaches out to our feelings and we enjoy the realisation that the Lord is in us, but it is not always so. An attack of indigestion can have the strangest effect upon our spiritual life, so far as our consciousness is concerned. The slightest little thing can come along and change the whole situation if we allow ourselves to go out into *things*. What things the enemy put up, to draw us out into them! He is busy setting traps everywhere, contriving situations all round us, always ready with something to upset us. How cleverly arranged it is, just at the time when we are least wanting to be upset. Go home from a time with the Lord amongst His people, feeling gloriously uplifted, and probably when you get across the doorstep there is something waiting for you!

How are you going to outwit the Devil, outmaneuver him, defeat him? By not going out into things. It is not easy; but not to go out into things, not to be drawn into the realm of the old creation so as to become involved in it, but to stand upon the ground that the adversary has to meet the perfection of Christ, is the sure way of his defeat, though we may have to bear with the difficult situation, and endure the pain and pang of it for quite a considerable time. But our position is that Christ is more than that, Christ in us is stronger than that, and falling back upon faith within, reaching out to Christ within as equal to this situation, we must repudiate it. David comes to our rescue so much in this realm. You will remember that on one occasion he was saying all sorts of depressing, hopeless things because the situation looked so utterly impossible; and then he recollected himself and said, "...This is my infirmity; but I will remember the years of the right hand of the Most High" (Psalm lxxvii. 10). To-day I have blue spectacles on! This is my way of viewing things! This is how things affect me! This is me, it is not the Lord! Let us attribute things to their right quarter, and give to Caesar the things that are Caesar's, and to God the things that are God's.

I am certain that here is the key to everything; the key to everything is Christ in you, Christ in me, Christ in His Body, and that to be lived upon by faith. It is the key to the superior wisdom, to outwit and outmatch the enemy. He will be defeated if we live on Christ and refuse to live on our own ground. The Lord make it clear to us.

Fifteen

The Man Whom
He Hath Ordained

*Reading: Romans viii. 29; Galatians iv. 19; Ephesians ii. 15, 16;
I Corinthians i. 24-30; xii. 13; Galatians iii. 27, 28; Acts xvii. 31.*

*"Inasmuch as he hath appointed a day in which he will
judge the world in righteousness by the man whom he
hath ordained; whereof he hath given assurance unto all
men, in that he hath raised him from the dead" (Acts
xvii. 31).*

The words "the man whom he hath ordained" take us back to
the point where we commenced our contemplation of things, into the
counsels of God before times eternal. It was then that the Man was
ordained. The history of this world, then, is to be gathered up, to be
summed up in that Man; its destiny is to be determined in Him.

Let us make a few comprehensive, and yet quite concrete statements in relation to this fact.

Firstly, *God's explanation of the universe is a Man*. If we want
to know the meaning of the universe, we must look at a Man: and if
we look at that Man whom He hath ordained, and see Him with the
eyes of our hearts enlightened, through a spirit of wisdom and revelation in the knowledge of Him, we shall see Him as God's explanation of the universe.

Secondly, *God's answer to everything that has resulted from
Adam's fall is a Man*. That is comprehensive. It is quite beyond our
working out; but it does not matter at what point you touch the out-
come of Adam's fall, or what phase of the result you touch, you will

find that God answers in a Man, in this Man. You may take any one of the issues of the fall as you see them expressed at different points, representing a state full of difficulty, full of complexity, full of tragedy apparently, and ask, "How is this to be dealt with, to be remedied?" God's answer is a Man, and this Man whom He hath ordained.

I do not want to launch out upon a course of illustration, but I will give you one example of what I mean by this. Take Babel. Now Babel is a problem: the scattering of the people, the confounding of the language, and all the result of Babel in nations and diversities of tongues, with all the weakness that issues from that—a determined and intended weakness—is a problem of considerable magnitude. It was a sovereign act of God, against a certain kind of strength which would take charge of the world apart from God. But Babel itself represents a very big problem, and a complex state of things, as being in itself something which God never intended. It is the outworking of the fall, and the expression of a curse. It has to be dealt with. The whole thing has to be cleared up. It can never abide if God is to have things as He intended. What is the answer to Babel? It is a Man. It is this Man. All that situation, that confusion, that tragedy, that evil, will be eventually cleared up in a Man. There will be in that Man a unity of all that is divided and scattered. There will be in that Man a coming to one understanding. We have the earnest of all this now in Christ. There is such a thing as spiritual misunderstanding, and it does not matter whether we can understand one another in our human language or not, we can all understand by the Holy Spirit the same thing, and speak an inward language. There is a oneness of understanding, and the full assurance of understanding in Christ. I merely instance it and do not stay to work it out.

Thirdly, *God's proclamation to men, in respect of their salvation, their satisfaction, their fulness, is a Man.* We will break that up in a minute or two.

Fourthly, *God's object, in all His dealings with His own, is a Man.* The object of all the Lord's strange and mysterious dealings, and of all His painful dealings with His own, is a Man, and He is entirely governed by His view of that Man in all He does with us.

Nothing in all His dealings is something in itself, but it is all related. He has His eye all the time upon a Man, and He acts in relation to us with that Man in view.

No experience of ours, under the hand of God, is an incident by itself. It does not come into our lives because of this, or that, or something else as apart. If we go wrong, God does not chastise us for this or that as a thing in itself. God's chastisements are not incidental, are not detached, are not apart, but in relation to an object, the object in His eye, a Man.

God's dealings, not only with His own, but with the world, which are different kinds of dealings, are in relation to that Man. If we were able to recognise what that means, and apply it, bring it into the realm of applied truth, it would considerably help us in our everyday life.

Now in those statements we have comprehensively set forth God's object, the great governing reality. Everything is explained by a Man, and in a Man, and that Man interprets the history and the destiny of the universe. It could be put in other ways, and a great deal more from the Word of God could be cited to show how this is so, but we have to go on to break it up further.

GOD HAS NOT EVOLVED OR PRODUCED A RELIGION

God has not evolved or produced a religion, that is, a system of religious teaching and practice. That is where so many have gone astray, and, as a consequence, you get the clever and scholarly works on the religion of the Semites, and all that sort of thing. To these are added works on comparative religions, with Judaism and Christianity included. The whole matter is reduced to comparative values in the religions of the world, as to which is the best, and if it can be proved, as many have tried to show, that Judaism was better than all the ancient religions, and Christianity better than both ancient and modern religions, then it is to be concluded that Christianity is the religion for the world. This is a missing of the point. It is not a thing that we are likely to be caught in, but we have to recognise this truth for ourselves, and see where men have gone astray. God has not evolved or produced a religion: God has presented a Man.

GOD HAS NOT PRESENTED A SET OF THEMES

God has not presented us (in the first instance) with a set of truths, themes, subjects, although the Bible may be full of these. He has not presented us with them, but with a Man. We are never called upon to preach salvation to anybody: we are called upon to preach Christ, and the salvation that is in Christ Jesus: "...it was the good pleasure of God...to reveal his Son in me, that I might preach him among the Gentiles..." (Galatians i. 15, 16). Any truth, any doctrine, any theme, any subject which is not a revelation of Christ, and a ministration of Him, and which does not bring into Christ and make Christ Himself greater and fuller in the life, has missed its intention, has been divorced and separated from the purpose of God, and does not stand with God at all. God has not presented us, in the first instance, with a set of truths, themes, subjects, though there be found great themes in the Word of God, such as atonement, redemption, and the many others; He has presented us with a Man. Everything with God from eternity to eternity is inseparably bound up with a Man.

Perhaps you are wondering what is the practical value of saying such things. The practical value is this, that you never come into the meaning and value of the things, even should you deal with them all your life long, if they are taken as things in themselves. The only dynamic in any truth is the living Christ. Sanctification is Christ, even as justification is Christ. These are not things to be taken and stated, laid hold of and appropriated as things in themselves: *Christ* is made unto us sanctification and redemption.

Now one or two qualifying statements need to be made alongside of that. While it is true that God has not presented us, in the first instance, with truths, and so on, but with a Man; while it is true that God has not evolved religion, but presented a Man; while we are called to preach, not salvation, but the Saviour, we must remember that, even that, it is not with a Man officially that we have to do, but with what He is personally. By officially, we mean it is not the office that He occupies as Redeemer, Saviour, Mediator, or any other of the designations which may be given Him, representing His official work, with which we have to be concerned. That is not the first thing, but the Man Himself. We are not saved by coming to Him in His official capacity as Saviour, we are saved by vital union with Him as a person.

It is not by our objective vision of the Man that we receive all God's meaning. There is great meaning and great value in Christ, viewed objectively; that is, as having summed up in Himself all that we need, and our holding fast by the fact of the completeness of everything in Christ. There is a real value for the heart in that, but it is not in having to do with the Man objectively alone, but subjectively, that we come into the Divine intention. The full hope of Christ is not Christ in salvation, but Christ in you. There are the values associated with Christ in salvation, but such a conception may be no more than of the official values of Christ as placed out there. The practical values of Christ are only known subjectively; they are what He is in Himself, and not what He is in office. You will see what we mean as we go on. It is very important for those of us who have responsibility in the things of God to recognise these differences.

Vital Union With Christ the Basis of God's Success

The point is this, that the basis of God's success is vital union with Christ, what we sometimes speak of as identification with Christ. God depends for His success entirely upon Christ within, and therefore, as we have said before, the one thing that God is after, and the one thing that the Devil is against, and will counter by every means of substitution, imitation, counterfeit, and so on, is getting Christ within men. Oh, how far things can go, and yet fall short of that! This is where the importance comes of recognising the difference between doctrine—even the doctrine of salvation—and the Man, the Person. We can preach the doctrine to men and get an assent, the consent of the mind to the doctrine, so that we have our catechumens, our classes for instructing converts in the doctrine; and when they have come to the place where they say, "Now I understand the doctrine, it is all clear to me now!" we think they are ready to be brought into the Church. The matter is much simpler than that;

and it must be more than that. You cannot educate anybody into the kingdom of God, not even with Christian doctrine. No one ever passes into the kingdom of God by understanding Christian doctrine intellectually. You may have all that, and yet have a serious breakdown before long. You may have an awful condition amongst your so-called converts in the face of all that. It may be found in the long run that they were never really saved, though they were baptised on the grounds that they understood all that you could say to them about Christian doctrine. Thus, on the one hand, perfectly honest people may make a grave mistake, and, on the other hand, the Devil is out to give a tremendous amount of what comes just short of new birth. He will readily allow things to go so far, provided they do not go that far. But once that thing is really done, you have the basis for everything. You have the basis for the doctrine in a living way, the basis of complete assurance, the basis for everything, once Christ is within. God's objective is reached with regard to the starting point, and everything is possible. That is what I mean by the difference between doctrine and the Person, between the official and the personal. The basis of God's success is Christ in you, union with Christ, identification with Christ in an inward way. This is laid down in the Word of God as the principle upon which God works in this dispensation from first to last.

THE PERFECTION OF THE DIVINE PROVISION SEEN IN RELATION TO:
(A) THE PROBLEM OF HUMAN LIFE

Let us take some of the passages to which we have referred at the commencement of our meditation, and see how they are but a following out of this very principle laid down as the basis upon which God works through this dispensation. Turn to Galatians iii. 28:

> *"There can be neither Jew nor Greek, there can be nei-*
> *ther bond nor free, there can be no male and female; for*
> *ye all are one man in Christ Jesus."*

This is the way in which God solves the problem of human life. As we find human life on this earth to-day, it really is a problem. It is up against that problem that all those well-intentioned people who have round-table conferences of an International character always come. You call your round-table conference, and you have your representatives of the different nations of the earth, East and West, North and South; you have your different representatives of the social realm, your working man, as he is called, and your aristocrat, your capitalist, the employer and the employee; and in order to get different points of view, you will have your male and your female. You laboriously work: a proposition is made, but someone from the other end of the earth cannot accept that; it is not suitable to their realm of life, to what obtains in their nation. Then, of course, the employee cannot bring himself to see the point of view of the employer, neither the employer the point of view of the employee; and there is not a little difficulty in a man seeing a woman's point of view. How many round tables have been held, and how many of them have been successful? The amazing thing is how men go on with their conferences! As long as we have been living, men have been having conferences, and what is the upshot? Every one gets just so far, and then there is deadlock. But they will have another one, and they will go on to the end trying to solve the problem of human life on that level of discussion, of conference.

Now God is perfectly aware of the whole situation. He is far more aware of the difficulties and the problems than anyone else. From His standpoint there are a great many more factors and features in the whole situation than have ever been manifested to men. But He has a solution, an infallible solution, and one which has fully proved itself wherever received. What is God's solution to the problem of human life? It is a Man.

(B) THE PROBLEM OF RACE

Here we have it: "...neither Jew nor Greek...." That is the national problem. If you are familiar with the background of Galatians, you know that it was a national problem that gave rise to that letter. Jewish believers were assuming a status above other believers. They were saying, "Well, we are the Jews, and they are the Greeks; we stand in one realm and they in another! We, as the Jews, have certain privileges and advantages, which they have not: we stand in a

more favoured position than they do; we are altogether superior!"
Greeks or Gentiles are spoken of by Jews as "the dogs," the out-
siders. How are you going to deal with the national problem? You
will never finally solve that problem by a round-table conference. It
is that problem which is so pressing the world to-day, between the
superior and the inferior races, between those who have the advantage and those who have not the advantage.

God's solution to the problem is a Man. In Christ there can be
neither Jew nor Greek. Has not the Man solved the problem? You and
I who come on to the ground of the Heavenly Man, who forsake the
earthly ground, forsake the national ground, and come on to the
ground of Christ, find blessed fellowship. Oh, what perfect fellowship! What profitable fellowship! What prospects loom up in view;
how fruitful it all is! So far from being a way of a loss, it is blessed-
ly full of value. What a tragedy that even so many of the Lord's own
people have not forsaken national ground. What prejudices and
implied limitations there are through pride. How they limit, how they
blight, how they keep out the fulness of Christ, and make God's
intention impossible. Get off that ground on to the ground of God's
Heavenly Man, where there can be neither Jew nor Greek, and the
national problem, as a part of the human problem, is solved.

(c) THE SOCIAL PROBLEM

Then further it is said, "...there can be neither bond nor
free...." The social problem is dealt with, the problem of the master
and the slave. How are you going to solve the problem of the
employer and the employee? You will only solve it in the Man, but in
Him you will solve it in truth. Then, if the Jew thinks that nationally he has an advantage over the Greek, and if the master thinks he
has an advantage over the servant, and, as is often the case, particularly in the East, the man thinks he has the advantage over the
woman, how are you to get over these problems? God's salvation is
a Man. You do not, of course, get rid of the facts; the distinctions are
not abolished here on the earth—and God forbid that we should
attempt such a thing—but on the ground of the "new man" we are
made as one. There we meet on a different ground altogether. *In*

Christ there can be neither Jew nor Greek, neither male nor female, neither bond nor free, neither superior nor inferior: advantages and disadvantages disappear.

(D) THE RELIGIOUS PROBLEM

The Apostle refers again to both the national and social problems, as you notice, in Colossians iii. 11, but he also expands a little: "Where there cannot be Greek and Jew, circumcision and uncircumcision...." Here he is perhaps putting his finger a little more firmly upon the Jew and the Greek problem. He is now stressing, not only the national, but the religious problem. How acute that was. In Christ there is no religious advantage over others; no one is in a position of less advantage on religious grounds than others. Then he speaks of barbarian and Scythian. This is a further reference to the racial question. These represent different levels of civilisation and cultivation, and the Apostle is clearing up the problem by saying that in Christ such distinctions have no place.

(E) THE PROBLEM OF HUMAN DESTINY

Then another aspect of this is brought before us in the passage in First Corinthians i. 24, 30:

"But unto them that are called, both Jews and Greeks,
Christ the power of God, and the wisdom of God....But
of him are ye in Christ Jesus, who was made unto us wis-
dom from God, and righteousness and sanctification, and
redemption."

Here is another problem, that of human destiny, and this is gathered up into two words, and words that are frequently repeated, wisdom and power, power and wisdom. The question here at Corinth is a reflex of Greek philosophy, which had crept in with its subtle and pernicious suggestions. The question is that of reaching the super-man status. That is the question of philosophy—the highest wisdom and the greatest power. Wisdom and power are the two constituents of the super-man. Philosophy has always had in view the thought of man reaching his destiny, the idea that man has a great destiny. Man has indeed a meaning, a great meaning; there is bound up with man a great idea. With many of the Pagans, the idea was that of the deification of humanity, of man slowly evolving until he becomes deified. So that the great man is to be worshipped. Their heroes were worshipped as approximating to their ideal, and this was all a movement toward the ultimate deification of humanity, and the characteristics of this supreme super-man, as thus conceived of, were wisdom and power. They were always stretching out for a superior wisdom to bring them into a place of superior power, and thus to realise the great destiny of man. The problem of human destiny was dealt with in the light of wisdom and power.

That lies behind the world to-day. Is it not this that we are meeting with now in dictators, in men who would dominate the world? It is a case of wisdom and power reaching such an attitude of human status that everything is brought under the dictator's dominion. He is regarded as the embodiment of the world's highest wisdom and greatest power. That is man. Such will be the Devil's man on the human level.

The question of human destiny is quite a living one for us. It is just as real and important and right a question for believers as it is for the world. It is not the world which is really in line with the destiny of man. There is no getting away from the fact that man has a marvellous destiny. God created man with an object far greater than anything the princes of this world have ever conceived, and so the question of human destiny is a right and a proper one, and perhaps one of the greatest. But the question which goes with it is, "How is the end to be reached?" Wisdom is quite right. This "one new man" is to display the manifold wisdom of God unto all supernatural intelligences, to be the embodiment of Divine wisdom on all its sides. Power is quite right. There is no doubt at all that this one "new man" is to be the instrument of the exercise of the infinite power of God, to be a display of God's mighty power. These things are a right consideration for us: they present a legitimate question, the problem of how to reach the super-man status. That was the question with the Greeks all the time. The answer of God through His Word is a Man whom He hath ordained. The answer is Christ within, the power and the wisdom. Christ within, in the power of death and resurrection, solves the problem of human destiny.

This world has tried to solve this problem by numerous systems of philosophy. If you sit down to investigate any one of them, you will find it is an attempt to solve the problem of human destiny, the meaning of man, and the meaning of the universe, and how man and the universe are to reach their predestined end. The world is full of systems of philosophy which are seeking to answer this question. The Lord answers it in a simple and direct way, and says that the solution to the problem is a Man, and that Man, in the power of death and resurrection, dwelling within. How are you and I to realise God's predestined purpose? This is the answer: "...Christ in you, the hope of glory" (Colossians i. 27). But this is Christ within as the wisdom and power of God. This wisdom is so simple. What does Christ within mean in relation to that great ultimate purpose of God? It is the earnest of that to which the Apostle by the Spirit elsewhere gives expression: "...foreordained to be conformed to the image of his Son..." (Romans viii. 29), and again: "...until Christ be formed in you..." (Galatians iv. 19). When that is done the world will be occupied by a great corporate Man of God's own kind, and the end will be reached. That Man is Christ, in His fulness—His Body.

How then are you going to solve these problems? Well, Plato will tell you all about it in his Republic! Oh, the laws and the regulations! Oh, the observances! See all that you have to take account of, to do, and not do, to institute, and carry out. It is all a tremendous system to bring man up to standard. The Lord's answer is a very much simpler one than that. Let Christ but dwell within, and He will work to bring you up to His own level. Give Him a chance within, and you will be conformed to His image; Christ will be fully formed in you. And when that is true of the whole Body, you have the one new, universal Man. Is that not wisdom? Oh, the poor philosophers! How they have exhausted their brains, and many of them have gone mad in the attempt to solve the problem of human destiny. The Lord's wisdom is so simple. Christ in you is the wisdom of God. That is how the whole problem is met. You have not to think everything out, plan it all, work to a colossal system of rules and regulations and observances; you have simply to let the Lord within have His way, and the end is sure. The problem of the universe is solved without any mental exhaustion. It is a matter of life. The foolishness of God is wiser than men, and the wisdom of God so simple. Men are spending the centuries wearing themselves out, and what is the result? Look at it to-day. What a sad picture of the upward progress of humanity! But God is effecting His purpose, and in the unseen there is a Man growing that is to fill the universe. God's way is so simple and so effective. If you want to solve the question of wisdom and power, this is it. Wisdom is the question of "how." Then it becomes a question of ability when you know how. Christ within is both the "how," and the "ability."

All this, and much more (the Word is full of it and we shall never exhaust it all) comes back to the one thing: *all things in Christ.* God's answer to everything, God's explanation of everything, God's means of realising everything is a Man, "the man Christ Jesus" (KJV). When this world has run its evil course, this inhabited earth will be judged *in* a Man. Men will be judged by what their inward relationship is to that Man. The question at the judgment will never be of how much good or bad, right or wrong, more or less, is in a man; it will turn upon this one point, "Are you in Christ?" If not, more or less makes no difference. God's intention, God's proclamation is that all things are in His Son. Are you in Him? Why not? The basis of judgment is very simple. It is all gathered up in a Man, and what is in that Man of God for us. That is the basis of judgment. It all comes back to the very simple, and yet comprehensive and blessed truth, that it is what Christ is that satisfies God, reaches God's end, and meets all our need. It is all summed up in a Man, "the man Christ Jesus" (KJV).

The Lord continue to open our eyes to see His glorious and Heavenly Man, who is also the Divine Servant.

Also by
T. Austin Sparks

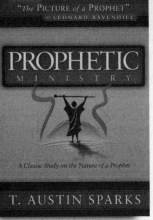

PROPHETIC MINISTRY

What is God's purpose for His Church today? How can believers know and fulfill that purpose? The Old Testament records God's desire for a people who would express His presence among the nations. He would be their King in a Kingdom marked by spiritual vision and holy living. Prophets in that time constantly challenged the people toward these ideals and warned of God's judgment when they disobeyed. Then— good news! Through Jesus, God made His Kingdom available to everyone, regardless of age, background, race, or training. As each believer responds to the enlightening, cleansing, and purifying work of the Holy Spirit, the Church can once again proclaim God's presence among the nations of the world!

ISBN: 0-9677402-4-X

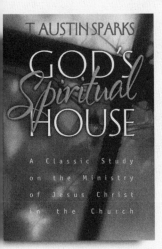

GOD'S SPIRITUAL HOUSE

In a time when everyone is trying to rediscover the Church, a voice comes to us from the past that shines like a great light in our utter darkness. In *God's Spiritual House* Sparks speaks out with compelling force that man cannot redefine the Church until Christ has come to repossess the Church. God's house is not a denomination, it is not a network, it is not a building, and it is not an organization. It is Christ Himself in undivided oneness found in all those in whom He really dwells.

ISBN: 0-9707919-0-9

Available at your local Christian bookstore.

Additional copies of this book and other book titles from DESTINY IMAGE are available at your local bookstore.

For a complete list of our titles, visit us at www.destinyimage.com Send a request for a catalog to:

Destiny Image® Publishers, Inc.

P.O. Box 310
Shippensburg, PA 17257-0310

"Speaking to the Purposes of God for This Generation and for the Generations to Come"